MIX
Papier aus verantwortungsvollen Quellen
Paper from responsible sources
FSC® C105338

Christian Deger

Behind the Curve

An Analysis of the Investment Behavior
of Private Equity Funds

Deger, Christian: Behind the Curve: An Analysis of the Investment Behavior of Private Equity Funds, Hamburg, Diplomica Verlag GmbH

Umschlaggestaltung: Diplomica Verlag GmbH, Hamburg
Covermotiv: © buchachon - Fotolia.com

ISBN: 978-3-8428-8910-1

© Diplomica Verlag GmbH, Hamburg 2013

Bibliografische Information der Deutschen Nationalbibliothek:
Die Deutsche Nationalbibliothek verzeichnet diese Publikation in der Deutschen Nationalbibliografie; detaillierte bibliografische Daten sind im Internet über http://dnb.d-nb.de abrufbar.

Die digitale Ausgabe (eBook-Ausgabe) dieses Titels trägt die ISBN 978-3-8428-3910-6 und kann über den Handel oder den Verlag bezogen werden.

Dieses Werk ist urheberrechtlich geschützt. Die dadurch begründeten Rechte, insbesondere die der Übersetzung, des Nachdrucks, des Vortrags, der Entnahme von Abbildungen und Tabellen, der Funksendung, der Mikroverfilmung oder der Vervielfältigung auf anderen Wegen und der Speicherung in Datenverarbeitungsanlagen, bleiben, auch bei nur auszugsweiser Verwertung, vorbehalten. Eine Vervielfältigung dieses Werkes oder von Teilen dieses Werkes ist auch im Einzelfall nur in den Grenzen der gesetzlichen Bestimmungen des Urheberrechtsgesetzes der Bundesrepublik Deutschland in der jeweils geltenden Fassung zulässig. Sie ist grundsätzlich vergütungspflichtig. Zuwiderhandlungen unterliegen den Strafbestimmungen des Urheberrechtes. Die Wiedergabe von Gebrauchsnamen, Handelsnamen, Warenbezeichnungen usw. in diesem Werk berechtigt auch ohne besondere Kennzeichnung nicht zu der Annahme, dass solche Namen im Sinne der Warenzeichen- und Markenschutz-Gesetzgebung als frei zu betrachten wären und daher von jedermann benutzt werden dürften. Die Informationen in diesem Werk wurden mit Sorgfalt erarbeitet. Dennoch können Fehler nicht vollständig ausgeschlossen werden und die Diplomica GmbH, die Autoren oder Übersetzer übernehmen keine juristische Verantwortung oder irgendeine Haftung für evtl. verbliebene fehlerhafte Angaben und deren Folgen.

Vorwort

Sehr geehrter Leser,

im Jahre 2010 entschloss sich der Bundesverband Alternative Investments e. V. (BAI), wissenschaftliche Arbeiten im Bereich der sog. Alternativen Investments zu fördern. Zu diesem Zweck wurde damals der BAI-Wissenschaftspreis ins Leben gerufen.

Einer der Hauptgründe sowie die Intention für diese Förderung waren und sind, dass das Wissen über Alternative Investments sowohl in der Breite als auch in der Tiefe leider immer noch sehr rudimentär ist. In weiten Teilen der Öffentlichkeit, der Politik, der Medien, aber auch auf Seiten der Investoren herrschen oftmals vielfache Missverständnisse hinsichtlich Nutzen und Risiken von Alternative Investments. Mit dem Wissenschaftspreis will der BAI einen Anreiz für Studenten und Wissenschaftler in Deutschland schaffen, Forschungsarbeit in diesem für institutionelle Investoren zukünftig immer wichtiger werdenden Bereich zu leisten.

Viele deutsche Hochschulen erklärten sich auf Anhieb bereit, den BAI bei der Bekanntmachung des Wissenschaftspreises zu unterstützen. Daraus resultierend erreichten den BAI zahlreiche anspruchsvolle Bewerbungen in den vier Kategorien „Dissertationen", „Master-/Diplomarbeiten", „Bachelorarbeiten" und „Sonstige Wissenschaftliche Arbeiten". Für diese wurde jährlich neben einem Award ein Preisgeld von 10.000 Euro an die Gewinner ausgelobt.

Wir freuen uns sehr, dass der Diplomica Verlag die Reihe „Alternative Investments" ins Leben gerufen hat. Diese Publikation wird sicherlich auch dazu beitragen, das Thema Alternative Investments einer Vielzahl von Personen näherzubringen.

Wir wünschen dem Leser nun eine spannende Lektüre!

Ihr
Bundesverband Alternative Investments e. V.

Table of Contents

List of Abbreviations 9

List of Symbols 10

List of Figures 11

List of Tables 12

List of Appendices 13

1 Introduction 15

2 Leveraged Buyout Transactions 17
    2.1 Legal Structure of Buyout Funds 18
    2.2 Mechanics of a Leveraged Buyout Transaction 20

3 Capital Structure and Pricing in Buyouts 23
    3.1 Principal Agent Driven Theories 23
        3.1.1 Principal Agent Conflicts on Company Level 23
        3.1.2 Principal Agent Conflicts on Investor Level 25
    3.2 Determinants beyond the Principal Agent Conflict 35
        3.2.1 Debt Market Conditions 35
        3.2.2 Reputation of the Private Equity Firm 36
        3.2.3 Other Determinants of Leverage and Pricing 37

4 Fund State and Investment Pressure 39
    4.1 Fund Performance 39
    4.2 Capital Invested 40
    4.3 Investment Pressure and Hypotheses 40

5 Data Description 43
    5.1 Sample Characteristics and Representativeness 44
    5.2 Explanatory Variables 48
        5.2.1 Fund Performance Variable 48

5.2.2 Capital Invested Variable	50
5.2.3 Investment Pressure Variables	50
5.2.4 Reputation Variables	51
6 Results	**53**
6.1 Basic Regression	53
6.2 Capital Invested Hypothesis	56
6.3 Fund Performance Hypothesis	58
6.4 Reputation Effects Hypothesis	64
7 Conclusion	**67**
Appendix	**69**
References	**75**

List of Abbreviations

AUM:	Assets under Management
CEO:	Chief Executive Officer
CI:	Capital Invested
EBITDA:	Earnings before Interest, Taxes, Depreciation & Amortization
EV:	Enterprise Value
FCF:	Free Cash Flow
GP:	General Partner
ICB:	Industry Classification Benchmark
IRR:	Internal Rate of Return
LP:	Limited Partner
LPA:	Limited Partnership Agreement
M&A:	Mergers & Acquisitions
NPV:	Net Present Value
PE:	Private Equity
PIK:	Payment-in-Kind
SPV:	Special Purpose Vehicle

List of Symbols

T_i:	Point of time in fund lifecycle with $i \in \{0, 1, 2, 3\}$
L:	Low state
H:	High state
q:	Probability of the occurrence of the high state
B:	Bad firm
G:	Good firm
α:	Probability of the arrival of a good firm
α_H:	Probability of the arrival of a good firm in the high state
α_L:	Probability of the arrival of a good firm in the low state
p:	Probability of a bad firm turning good
I:	Amount of capital needed to invest into a target firm
x:	Cash flow from investments
Z:	Resulting cash flow from the investment into a good firm
F:	Face value of debt
K:	Amount of capital invested by investors
$w_{GP}(x)$:	Fund manager security
$w_I(x)$:	Investor security
$w_{P,i}(x_i)$:	Ex post security for the mixed financing strategy with $i \in \{1, 2\}$
S:	Threshold for carry region
k:	Profit share for investor

List of Figures

Figure 1: Accumulated value of worldwide leveraged buyouts (in $bn) 17
Figure 2: Fundraising of European buyout funds by type of investor 19
Figure 3: Mechanics of a leveraged buyout 21
Figure 4: Order of cash distribution in leveraged buyout funds 22
Figure 5: Timeline of the Axelson et al. model 26
Figure 6: Investment behavior in the pure ex post financing case for T_1 and T_2 28
Figure 7: Investment behavior with pure ex post (P), pure ex ante (A) and mixed (M) financing 31
Figure 8: Payoff structure of GP and LP securities 34
Figure 9: EBITDA multiple, debt ratio and debt / EBITDA over time 45
Figure 10: Median money multiple by fund age in years 46
Figure 11: Median capital invested ratio by fund age in years 47
Figure 12: Calculation of performance variables 49

List of Tables

Table 1: Payoff scenarios under full ex post financing (One period model) 27
Table 2: Strategies under pure ex ante financing 29
Table 3: Summary statistics of dataset 44
Table 4: Transaction financials at entry 45
Table 5: Investment performance statistics 46
Table 6: Fund performance variable summary statistics 49
Table 7: Capital invested variable summary statistics 50
Table 8: Reputation statistics at entry date 52
Table 9: Basic Regression Results 55
Table 10: Capital Invested Regression Results 57
Table 11: Performance Regression Results 61
Table 12: Interaction Regression Results 63
Table 13: Reputation Regression Results 65
Table 14: Long Term Reputation Regression Results 72
Table 15: Reputation Dummy Regression Results 73
Table 16: Additive Long Term Reputation Regression Results 74

List of Appendices

Appendix 1: Industry reference table 69
Appendix 2: Time series data 70
Appendix 3: Fund statistics 71
Appendix 4: Regression results 72

1 Introduction

In aviation, getting "behind the power curve" usually refers to a situation in which an aircraft is flying slowly at low altitude and there is not enough power to reestablish a controlled flight. The only option for the pilot to recover from this situation is to nose dive the aircraft in order to regain airspeed.[1] In private equity, especially in the field of leveraged buyouts, fund managers are regularly confronted with a less dangerous, but similar situation. Facing low fund performance or having an overhang of uninvested capital puts fund managers "behind the curve" and requires measures for recovery. This study investigates the behavior of fund managers exposed to this kind of distressed situation, by analyzing the effects on both financing structure and pricing of portfolio investments.

In the domain of corporate acquisitions, leveraged buyouts (LBO) have gained tremendous importance since their first appearance in the late 1970's. After having suffered from different economic downturns throughout the years, buyouts have become a major force in the world-wide economy and reached a record accumulated transaction value of $878bn in the year 2007.[2] LBOs are generally conducted by a private equity (PE) firm through a buyout fund. The fund manager raises a certain amount of equity from outside investors and invests it into later-stage companies for an average holding period of around five years.[3] An important characteristic of an LBO is that investments are not only financed by equity capital from the fund, but also with a significant amount of debt, which is raised individually on a deal-by-deal basis. Moreover, the compensation of both fund managers and equity investors is not based on the individual investment itself, but on the success of the whole fund.[4] As a result, the particular conditions of buyout investments in a fund setting as well as the distinct incentive structure of buyout funds facilitate an increased sensitivity of fund managers with regard to the current state of their fund. This may also influence their leverage and pricing decisions on the transaction level.

Corresponding research on buyout structuring is still in its infancy. While there is an increasing amount of empirical literature on the various determinants of leverage and pricing in buyout transactions,[5] comparatively little is known about how the investment behavior of buyout funds drives these structuring decisions. A notable exception is the work by Axelson, et al. (2009), who develop a theoretical model that is based on a principal agent conflict between fund managers and outside investors. The model provides a number of predictions on how the investment behavior of fund managers impacts leverage and pricing decisions at investment entry.[6]

---

[1] See Klaas (2008), p. 1.
[2] Data based on Thomson One Banker.
[3] See Strömberg (2007), p. 37.
[4] See Pindur (2007), pp. 33ff.
[5] See Axelson, et al. (2010); Demiroglu / James (2010); Ivashina / Kovner (2008).
[6] See Axelson, et al. (2009), pp. 1550f.

The main goal of this study is to identify the forces behind these decisions and to empirically verify the predictions of the Axelson, et al. (2009) model. Therefore, the work of Axelson, et al. (2009), supplemented with additional literature on LBO leverage and pricing as well as the investment behavior of buyout funds, forms the theoretical part of the study. Based on the findings of this theoretical part, three hypotheses are formulated and empirically tested using comprehensive investment pressure variables developed from a representative dataset of 1,190 buyout transactions, which were completed between 1985 and 2009. The results obtained from this analysis suggest the existence of a significant difference regarding the transaction structure between funds that are "above" and funds that are "behind the curve".

The remainder of the study is structured as follows. Chapter 2 describes the organizational structure of buyout funds as well as the general mechanics of an LBO. Chapter 3 presents the most prevalent theories regarding capital structure and pricing of buyout transactions. Chapter 4 introduces different measures to assess the current state of a buyout fund and formulates three testable hypotheses. While chapter 5 describes the dataset as well as the formation of the investment pressure variables, the hypotheses are empirically tested using multivariate regression models in chapter 6. Chapter 7 concludes.

2 Leveraged Buyout Transactions

In a leveraged buyout, a private equity firm acquires a later-stage company using a significant amount of debt and a relatively small portion of equity to finance the transaction.[7] Leveraged buyouts first appeared in the 1970's and became an important phenomenon at the latest by 1989, when the private equity firm and LBO pioneer Kohlberg Kravis & Roberts (KKR) acquired RJR Nabisco for a total transaction value of $31bn[8], still being one of the largest LBO transactions to date.[9] As a result of the increasing popularity of this special type of corporate acquisition, in 1989 Michael C. Jensen predicted leveraged buyouts to become the predominant organizational form throughout the corporate world.[10] However, shortly thereafter LBO activity plummeted as a result of a crash in the junk bond market and the associated defaults of numerous private equity backed firms. Throughout the 1990's, the buyout market recovered and private equity firms raised a record amount of more than $850bn in 2007.[11] Again, this second boom was abruptly stopped and came to an end in the course of the financial crisis of 2008 – 2009 and the associated tightening credit market conditions.[12]

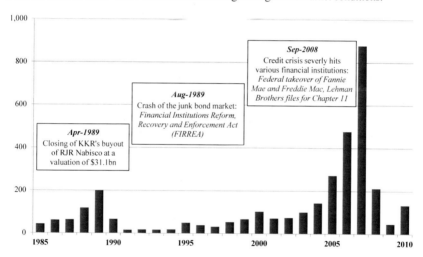

Figure 1: Accumulated value of worldwide leveraged buyouts (in $bn)[13]

---

[7] As opposed to venture capital firms, which focus on early-stage ventures, private equity firms focus their investments on established, later-stage companies.
[8] See Atlas (2001), p. 1; In 1989 USD.
[9] There have been LBO deals between 2006 and 2007 that were nominally larger. Adjusted for inflation though, none of these deals exceeded the total transaction value of the RJR Nabisco deal.
[10] See Jensen (1989), p. 64.
[11] From both ex ante and ex post investors. Based on data from Thomson One Banker.
[12] See Kaplan / Strömberg (2009), p. 122.
[13] Own illustration. Data based on Thomson One Banker.

To set the ground for this study's analysis on the investment behavior of private equity funds, the next chapters will describe their general structure as well as important mechanics of a leveraged buyout transaction.

2.1 Legal Structure of Buyout Funds

Private equity firms raise capital through a private equity fund, which is usually organized as limited partnership, with the fund managers serving as general partners (GP) and equity investors as limited partners (LP). These limited partnerships are typically organized for a fixed term of about 10 years.[14] While the GPs are responsible for managing the fund and its investments, they are fully liable to the debts of the partnership. The LPs, however, are not actively involved in the management of the fund and are only liable to the extent of the amount of money they have invested. During the time of the fund's existence, the GP/LP relationship is governed by a limited partnership agreement (LPA), which regulates the rights and obligations of each party. Important regulations in a LPA are the timing and industry focus of investments, the compensation of the fund managers, the maximum amount of capital a LP is allowed to contribute to the fund, the drawdown process of committed capital as well as the distribution of returns.[15] In most cases, the LPA also forces the GPs to commit capital to the fund from their personal assets, in order to mitigate potential principal agent conflicts on investor level.[16]

In addition to the GP's personal capital commitment, there are numerous investors acting as LPs in a private equity transaction. Traditionally, the most important ones have been banks, pension funds, insurance companies as well as funds-of-funds. However, the composition of investor types which allocate their capital in private equity experienced quite a change during the 2008 – 2009 financial crisis. While many traditional LPs reduced their committed capital compared to previous years, especially governmental agencies became a major source of financing in the private equity market.

---

[14] See Metrick / Yasuda (2010), p. 2.
[15] See Blaydon / Wainwright (2003), pp. 2ff.
[16] See Kaplan / Strömberg (2009), p. 124.

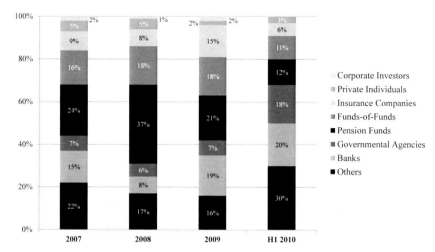

Figure 2: Fundraising of European buyout funds by type of investor[17]

LPs usually do not provide the full amount of their investment right at fund initiation but their committed capital is called by the fund managers in different tranches (drawdown). Investors have the strict obligation to serve these capital calls as default may severely damage the fund's investment timeline. If an investor lacks sufficient funds to serve his full commitment, the GPs usually steps in and tries to sell the LPs interest at a discount on a secondary market. If this approach is not successful, the GP may pose penalties on the respective LP, which might even lead to a full retention of his earlier investments.[18]

Debt financing is provided either by traditional banks or other institutions (e.g. hedge funds or insurance companies) and can be structured as senior or subordinated debt. Senior debt instruments, including A, B, C term loans and revolving credit as well as CAPEX facilities, generally have strict financial covenants, whereas subordinated debt comprehends instruments such as second lien notes and mezzanine financing, containing less and more lenient covenants.[19] During recent years, an increasing trend towards covenant-lite loans can be observed in buyout financing and new features such as payment-in-kind (PIK) toggles are replacing traditional debt financing instruments.[20]

---

[17] Based on data from EVCA (2010), p. 18.
[18] See Blaydon / Wainwright (2003), p. 3.
[19] See Achleitner, et al. (2010b), p. 12; Kaplan / Stein (1993), pp. 330 – 336.
[20] See Demiroglu / James (2010), p. 312.

2.2 Mechanics of a Leveraged Buyout Transaction

The process of a leveraged buyout transaction can be described based on four consecutive phases: Fund Raising & Investment Initiation, Deal Structuring & Entry, Monitoring, and Exit.[21]

Fund Raising & Investment Initiation During this phase, the GP establishes a buyout fund and raises capital from outside LPs. As described above, equity capital sources may comprise high net worth individuals as well as institutional investors. Once a pre-specified amount of capital has been committed by the LPs, the fund-raising GPs usually announce a first closing of the fund to drawdown the money raised so far and to start investing. Additional capital commitments are still possible until an upper limit is reached. During the investment period the fund is seeking to invest in companies which meet the criteria specified in the LPA. Once a potential target is identified, it is evaluated in a due diligence process, shedding light on various areas of the respective business. Especially for larger deals, the PE firm might engage external advisors in order to speed up this process.[22] If the assessment of the target company was successful and the GP is ready to invest, he steps into the next phase.

Deal Structuring & Entry In the Deal Structuring & Entry phase the financial structure and other investment details, such as corporate governance or management incentive schemes, are negotiated. This second phase is of particular importance with regard to this study, as it involves the fund manager's decision about financing structure and pricing. Once these issues have been resolved, the actual transaction takes place. Therefore, a "NewCo" is formed, a special purpose vehicle (SPV), which is fully owned by the private equity firm[23] and which seeks to acquire a controlling stake in the prospective portfolio company. The transaction is financed by both equity (contributed by investors) and debt, which is raised from traditional banks or other institutions.[24] Debt is collateralized by the target firm itself and is subject to common interest payments, which are usually serviced by the target company's cash flows. In return for its investment, the NewCo participates in the economic success of the portfolio company (Figure 3).

---

[21] Process adapted from Pindur (2007), pp. 33ff.
[22] Kaplan / Strömberg (2009), p. 124.
[23] Given the transaction is not conducted as a syndicated deal where multiple private equity companies may have a stake in the NewCo.
[24] See Pindur (2007), pp. 44f.

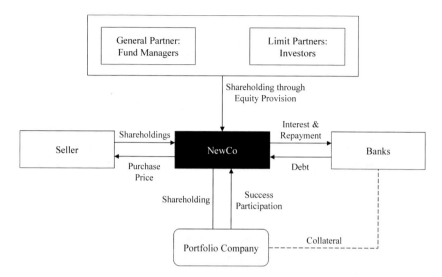

Figure 3: Mechanics of a leveraged buyout[25]

Monitoring During the holding period, the PE firm monitors the portfolio company and undertakes efforts to improve its efficiency. Commonly, these efforts can be categorized as financial, governance and operational engineering.[26] While the financial component of value creation is mainly attributable to the leverage effect of debt financing,[27] both governance and operational improvements partly comprise organizational changes within the company.[28]

Exit On average, a private equity company exits a buyout investment after four to five years.[29] This can happen through various exit channels such as an initial public offering (IPO), a trade sale or a secondary buyout. There is also a small fraction of buyout companies that file for bankruptcy and thus need to be written off by the PE firm.[30] The proceeds of the investment are divided among GPs and LPs as defined in the LPA. A typical order of cash distribution is depicted in Figure 4. First of all, the management fee to GPs is paid out. It usually ranges from 1.5 to 2.5% of the fund's committed capital and represents the compensation for initiation, development and management of the fund.[31] Secondly, LPs receive back their capital drawdowns including a preferred return (hurdle rate), usually ranging from 6 to 10%.[32] After management fee, drawdowns and preferred returns have been distributed, there

---

[25] Modified, based on Pindur (2007), p. 23.
[26] See Kaplan / Strömberg (2009), p. 131.
[27] See Achleitner, et al. (2010a), p. 3.
[28] See Kaplan / Strömberg (2009), p. 132.
[29] See Strömberg (2007), p. 37.
[30] See Strömberg (2007), p. 40; In his comprehensive study the author identified a bankruptcy rate of 6.2% across the LBO universe.
[31] See Blaydon / Wainwright (2003), p. 2; Metrick / Yasuda (2010), p. 45.
[32] See Metrick / Yasuda (2010), p. 12; Not all firms require a preferred return or hurdle rate to be paid out to LPs before the GP participates in the funds profits.

may be a carry catch-up region where the GP receives all proceeds of the fund before remaining profits are split between GPs and LPs according to the LPA. The final profit share of GPs is called carried interest (carry) and typically amounts to 20% of net profits.[33]

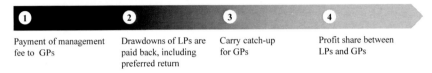

| Payment of management fee to GPs | Drawdowns of LPs are paid back, including preferred return | Carry catch-up for GPs | Profit share between LPs and GPs |

Figure 4: Order of cash distribution in leveraged buyout funds[34]

The compensation structure described above primarily serves to align the interests of fund managers and investors. However, the fact that the fund manager first has to earn back the full capital commitments of LPs before he participates in the fund's profits by himself, may cause an overinvestment problem especially in the later stage of a fund's lifecycle.[35] This is an important aspect when investigating the impact of investment pressure on a fund manager's behavior and is described in more detail in chapter 0.

---

[33] See Metrick / Yasuda (2010), p. 45.
[34] Own source.
[35] See Axelson, et al. (2009), p. 1560.

3 Capital Structure and Pricing in Buyouts

Even though, one of the most remarkable characteristics of an LBO is the high amount of outside debt used to finance the transaction, comparably little effort has been spent on explaining the financing structure of buyout investments. However, in order to interpret and predict the dynamics of the buyout industry, it is of essential importance to understand why private equity firms are leveraging their portfolio companies that heavily and which factors determine not only their usage of leverage but also their pricing decisions.

This chapter is introducing a selection of the most prevalent theories trying to answer these questions in the buyout context. In the first part of the chapter, the papers of Jensen (1989) and Axelson, et al. (2009) are introduced, shedding light on potential reasons for fund managers to finance their portfolio companies partially with debt. Additionally, it is elaborated on the implications on target pricing decisions by the buyout firm. The introduced theories within this part mainly focus on resolving principal agent conflicts by aligning the incentives of different parties. The second part presents different determinants of both debt level and pricing in buyouts beyond principal agent driven theories. Besides the papers of Axelson, et al. (2010), Ivashina / Kovner (2008) and Demiroglu / James (2010), which examine LBO specific factors, also a selection of traditional corporate finance theories is shortly introduced in order to account for other determinants.

3.1 Principal Agent Driven Theories

3.1.1 Principal Agent Conflicts on Company Level[36]

In his 1989 seminal paper, Michael C. Jensen discusses the increasing appearance of leveraged buyouts during the 80's. One of his major arguments for an "eclipse of the public corporation" is that private equity backed firms optimize their capital structure and thus exploit the positive effects of debt financing on their operations. Partly induced by regulations in response to the Great Depression in the 1930's,[37] institutional minority investors were kept off an active involvement in their portfolio companies. This left room for the development of large inefficiencies in public corporations and opened up the opportunity for less passive investors to recover the lost value. By delisting the target company, private equity funds escape the regulations imposed on public companies and are able to leverage the potential of a more active involvement. Jensen (1989) identifies two major reasons why increased debt financing has a positive effect on buyout companies.

---

[36] Unless otherwise stated, all thoughts in this paragraph are taken from Jensen (1989).
[37] See Jensen (1989), p. 65; Jensen directly mentions the Glass-Steagall Banking Act (1933), the Chandler Bankruptcy Revision Act (1938), and the Investment Company Act (1940).

Disciplining effect of debt The issuance of high amounts of debt requires a steady cash flow in order to serve interest and principal payments. Considering the fact that in a buyout transaction, debt is issued in exchange for equity,[38] Jensen describes debt as an effective substitute for dividends, a quasi-contractual distribution of a share of the free cash flow. However, other than with dividends, managers do not have the possibility to opportunistically cut down these frequent payouts and are therefore prevented from spending the free cash flow for potentially value destroying projects. Due to the fact that managers are forced to pay down the high debt burden, they are also encouraged to use the company's resources more efficiently as it is the case in a less financially distressed situation. This fact, in combination with the active involvement of the private equity investor, may lead to corporate restructuring in various forms such as the reduction of overhead or the disposal of unprofitable assets. Even though, buyout companies get into financial trouble more frequently, they less often file for bankruptcy compared to public companies. On the one hand this is a result of the existence of a usually financially strong private equity investor, which enables large equity injections when they are necessary. On the other hand, due to the comparably high leverage ratio, lending banks may intervene and try to preserve the remaining value of the company earlier as it is the case for companies, which have outstanding debt close to their liquidation value.

Higher equity ownership of management Another disciplining effect of debt, especially in leveraged buyout situations, arises from the associated shift in equity ownership at the management team's advantage. Kaplan / Strömberg (2009) analyzed 43 leveraged buyouts in the United States from 1996 to 2004 and found that the average ownership of chief executive officers (CEO) amounted to 5.4% post-LBO, a greater share than in public companies.[39] The higher equity ownership leads to a more efficient alignment of management's and shareholders' interests and thus to a more consequent execution of a shareholder value driven philosophy.

While the reasons for high leverage described by Jensen (1989) are rather derived from traditional financing theory and applied to the LBO context, Axelson, et al. (2009) approach the problem with a PE specific theoretical model, analyzing the relationship between ex ante financing by LPs and ex post debt financing. Due to the considerable attention the authors received from the corporate finance community[40] and to the paper's specific focus on leveraged buyout transactions, the model is explained in greater detail in the next section.

---

[38] Debt is issued to purchase the shares of existing investors.
[39] See Kaplan / Strömberg (2009), p. 131.
[40] See The Brattle Group (2011); The paper "Why Are Buyouts Levered? The Financial Structure of Private Equity Funds" was awarded the Brattle Group Prize for the best paper in corporate finance published in 2009. The Brattle Group Prizes are awarded annually for outstanding papers on corporate finance. The winning papers are chosen by the Associate Editors of The Journal of Finance.

3.1.2 Principal Agent Conflicts on Investor Level[41]

Axelson, et al. (2009) base their theory on principal agent conflicts between different parties. According to an optimal balancing of these conflicts, they develop distinct financing contracts in the context of leveraged buyout transactions. Besides proposing a new explanation for the financial structure of private equity funds, the theory also draws conclusions about GP/LP compensation as well as the cyclicality of the private equity industry.

The Setup

There are three different types of agents: The fund manager (GP), the investor (LP) and the fly-by-night operator. All agents are assumed to be risk neutral and have access to an investment opportunity yielding the risk-free rate. The theory is based on a three period model which is applicable independently from the financing strategy chosen by the GP.[42] The fund is initiated in T_0. In T_1 and T_2 all agents observe the respective state of the economy, which can be either good (H) or bad (L). Each period a target firm arrives, with the GP being the only agent that is able to assess its quality. A good firm (G) arrives with probability α and a bad firm (B) with $(1-\alpha)$, respectively. Depending on the respective state, there are two possible values for α, being α_H and α_L with $\alpha_H > \alpha_L$. The probability that α takes a value of α_H is q, and $(1-q)$ that it takes a value of α_L. At each arrival of a firm the GP decides whether or not to invest an amount I. An investment into a good firm results in a certain cash flow of $x = Z > 0$, while an investment into a bad firm results in $x = Z$ with probability p and $x = 0$ with probability $(1-p)$. Any cash flows from investments are not known by any party before T_3. However, it is known that an investment into a good firm yields a positive and an investment into a bad firm a negative net present value (NPV). This is defined by:

$$pZ < I < Z \qquad (1)$$

The GP is assumed not to have sufficient funds at his disposal to finance investments by himself. In order to raise capital from outside investors, he issues a security $w_I(x)$ collateralized by the cash flow x and keeps the residual claim $w_{GP}(x) = x - w_I(x)$. Both $w_I(x)$ and $w_{GP}(x)$ are non-decreasing in order to avoid moral hazard problems (monotonicity condition).

Furthermore, it is not possible for the GP to make a profit from raising outside capital and investing it into assets yielding the risk-free rate. If it was possible to make a positive profit from these passive strategies, the market would be swamped with an infinite number of fly-by-night operators. Since it would be impossible to establish an equilibrium in an economy where fly-by-night operators earn positive rents while investors are breaking even, fly-by-night operators are assumed to only find investments which yield a NPV below or equal to zero. Accordingly, the fly-by-night condition for invested capital K must be satisfied:

---

[41] Unless otherwise stated, all thoughts in this paragraph are taken from Axelson, et al. (2009).
[42] The different financing strategies are explained on pp. 12f.

Fly-by-night condition:

$$w_{GP}(x) = 0 \text{ whenever } x \leq K \qquad (2)$$

The fly-by-night condition forces the GP's profit only to become positive after the fund's investments have earned back the investors' initial capital outlay K. However, this leads to a convex return structure of $w_{GP}(x)$ and causes an asset substitution problem similar to the one described by Jensen / Meckling (1976) in the context of a shareholder-debt holder conflict.[43] Especially at the end of the fund lifecycle (in the described model by Axelson et al. this would be investments conducted in T_2), there are certain situations where the GP has the incentive to opportunistically take higher risk at the cost of outside investors. This asset substitution problem will be addressed in greater detail later in this section.

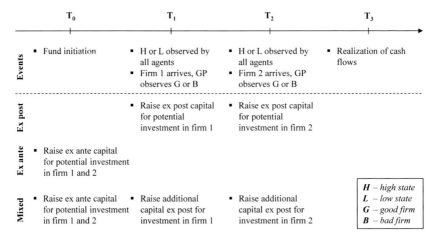

Figure 5: Timeline of the Axelson et al. model[44]

As indicated in Figure 5, there are three options for the GP to time capital raisings:

1. *Pure ex post financing*: Financing is acquired after fund initiation for each investment separately. Investor securities are backed by the individual cash flow of the respective deal.

2. *Pure ex ante financing:* Full financing is acquired before the first investment. Investor securities are backed by the cash flows of all investments made by the fund.

3. *Mixed financing:* Ex ante and ex post financing are combined. Investors providing ex ante capital have a claim against the sum of all cash flows, while the security of ex post capital providers is only backed by the cash flows from one specific investment.

---

[43] See Jensen / Meckling (1976), p. 315.
[44] Own source.

Subsequently, the different financing strategies are described in more detail and an optimal security design is derived for each of the three options. It will be shown that mixed financing is the most efficient strategy, setting the right incentives for all agents to decide according to a postulated equilibrium.

Pure ex post financing

In the pure ex post financing case, the GP does not raise any capital in T_0 but separately at each point in time when a potential target firm arrives. In order to identify an equilibrium for the dynamic two period model, a one period setting is analyzed in a first step.

As described above, to invest an amount I into a firm, the GP first has to raise capital from investors by issuing a security $w_I(x)$. Generally this security could be either equity or debt. However, due to the fly-by-night condition, both $w_I(I) = I$ and $w_{GP}(I) = 0$ have to hold. This is not given with a straight equity issue and thus leaves debt as the only possible security. Accordingly, in order to finance a potential investment, the GP issues debt with face value F, satisfying $I \leq F \leq Z$. To derive the optimal security design, it remains to be determined under which conditions outside investors are willing to provide financing. Table 1 depicts the five different payoff scenarios in a one period model.

		x	$w_I(x)$	$w_{GP}(x)$
1)	Raise no capital	0	0	0
2)	Raise capital and invest in good firm	Z	I	Z – I
3)	Raise capital and invest in bad firm which stays bad	0	0	0
4)	Raise capital and invest in bad firm which turns good	Z	I	Z – I
5)	Raise capital and store at risk-free rate	I	I	0

Table 1: Payoff scenarios under full ex post financing (One period model)[45]

For the GP, scenario 5 is strictly dominated by scenarios 3 and 4, leading to a simple rule for the one period model: If the GP receives financing, he invests independently of the firm's quality. If he does not receive financing, he does not invest at all.[46] However, investors only provide financing if they at least get back their initial investment. As a result, capital is only provided if the following break-even condition is met:[47]

$$(\alpha + (1-\alpha)p)Z \geq I \qquad (3)$$

---

[45] Own source.
[46] The GP always has the incentive to invest if his efforts to raise financing were successful. Otherwise he would receive a certain payoff of 0.
[47] Investors' break even condition is $(\alpha + (1 - \alpha)p)F \geq I$, which requires $(\alpha + (1 - \alpha)p)Z \geq I$ to be met so that financing is possible.

In addition to that, it is assumed that investors generally expect α to be too low to justify financing:

$$(E(\alpha) + (1 - E(\alpha))p)Z < I \qquad (4)$$

As a result of (4), ex post financing is never possible in the low state, and it is only possible if α_H is high enough. This is the static solution for the one period model. By applying an adapted form of the intuitive criterion according to Cho / Kreps (1987), one can show that the solution for the one period case is also an equilibrium for the two period model.

Given that α_H is high enough to satisfy investors' break even condition, the investment behavior in equilibrium for the pure ex post financing case is depicted in Figure 6. Both in T_1 and T_2 the GP will always invest in any firm in the high state and he will never be able to invest in the low state. Hence, there will always be inefficiencies from overinvestment in the high and underinvestment in the low state if the pure ex post financing strategy is applied.[48]

$$(E(\alpha_H) + (1 - E(\alpha_H))p)Z \geq I$$

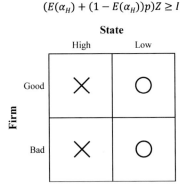

Figure 6: Investment behavior in the pure ex post financing case for T_1 and T_2[49]

Pure ex ante financing

In the pure ex ante case, the GP raises $2I$ at T_0 in order to independently decide whether to invest in the two subsequent periods. Therefore, he again issues a security $w_I(x)$, which is now, different from the ex post case, backed by the sum of all cash flows from both potential investment opportunities. Again, the investor security is senior to the GP security, leaving the fund manager with a residual claim on the aggregated cash flow of $w_{GP}(x) = x - w_I(x)$. In an optimal case without any inefficiency, the GP would only invest in good firms and store capital at the risk free rate if there are only bad firms available. However, due to the risk-shifting incentives provided by the fly-by-night condition, this first best solution is unachievable. In a situation, where the GP did not come across a good firm in T_1, he passes up the

---

[48] There will always be underinvestment if $(E(\alpha_H) + (1 - E(\alpha_H))p)Z < I$ as investors are not willing to provide financing even if there are high quality firms available.
[49] Based on Axelson, et al. (2009), p. 1557.

investment opportunity and stores an amount I at the risk free rate. In T_2 though, he always has an incentive to invest in a firm of any type as he would receive nothing otherwise. Bearing this asset substitution problem in mind, one can identify the strategies depicted in Table 2, given an amount $2I$ was raised in T_0.

	Resulting cash flow x
Good firm in T_1 & good firm in T_2	2Z
Good firm in T_1 & risk free rate in T_2	Z + I
Risk free rate in T_1 & good firm in T_2	Z + I
Risk free rate in T_1 & bad firm in T_2 which turns good	Z + I
Risk free rate in T_1 & bad firm in T_2 which stays bad	I

Table 2: Strategies under pure ex ante financing[50]

To develop a security design facilitating this behavior, $w_{GP}(x)$ needs to be maximized according to a maximization problem, which incorporates all the strategies from the table above:

$$\max_{w_{GP}(x)} E\big(w_{GP}(x)\big) = E(\alpha)^2 w_{GP}(2Z) + \big(2\,E(\alpha)(1 - E(\alpha))\big) + (1 - E(\alpha))^2 p)w_{GP}(Z + 1) \quad (5)$$

Four different conditions have to be considered when solving for $w_{GP}(x)$:

Monotonicity condition:

$$x - x' \geq w_{GP}(x) - w_{GP}(x') \geq 0 \text{ with } x > x' \quad (6)$$

Fly-by-night condition:

$$w_{GP}(x) = 0 \text{ if } x \leq 2I \quad (7)$$

Break-even condition:

$$E\big(x - w_{GP}(x)\big) \geq 2I \quad (8)$$

---

[50] Own source.

Incentive compatibility condition with pure ex ante financing:

$$E(\alpha) + (1 - E(\alpha))p)w_{GP}(Z + I) \geq \qquad (9)$$
$$((1 - p)E(\alpha) + 2p(1 - p)(1 - E(\alpha)))w_{GP}(Z) + p(E(\alpha) + (1 - E(\alpha))p)w_{GP}(2Z)$$

Monotonicity, fly-by-night and break-even condition follow the same rationale as before. The incentive compatibility condition makes sure that the GP only follows the strategies described in Table 2. The left hand side of the inequality describes a situation in which the GP passes up a bad firm in T_1 and invests into any firm in T_2. In case a bad firm arrives in T_1 passing up always has to be more attractive for the GP than investing, as covered by the right hand side of condition (9).[51]

The optimal security design that follows from solving the maximization problem under consideration of conditions (6) – (9) is given by

$$w_I(x) = \begin{cases} \min(x, F) & x \leq Z + I \\ F + k(x - (Z + I)) & x > Z + I \end{cases}$$

where $F \geq 2I$ and $k \in (k, 1]$ \qquad (10)

The derived return structure of the investor security is contingent on the level of payoffs realized by the whole fund and reflects common practice in LP compensation as described in chapter 2.2.

1. For cash flows below the provided amount of debt F, investors receive all of the cash flows.
2. For cash flows higher than F and below $(Z + I)$, the fund manager receives all of the cash flows after investors have received back their initial investment.
3. After both the GP and investors have received their claims from 1. and 2., cash flows above $(Z + I)$ are split between the two parties according to a factor k.

The derived security design incentivizes the GP to act fully efficient in T_1, only investing into good firms, independently from the state of the economy. However, not investing in T_1, leads to overinvestment in T_2 due to the risk-shifting incentive triggered by the fly-by-night condition. As depicted in Figure 7, in this situation ex post financing generates the more efficient outcome as it forces the GP only to invest in the high state, in which good firms are more likely to arrive due to the definition of $\alpha_H > \alpha_L$. This second best solution of the two period model can be achieved by combining ex post and ex ante financing to a mixed financing strategy.

---

[51] Axelson, et al. (2009) show that (9) implies all other necessary conditions and thus is a sufficient condition for incentive compatibility.

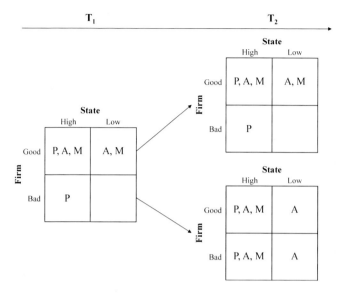

Figure 7: Investment behavior with pure ex post (P), pure ex ante (A) and mixed (M) financing[52]

Mixed financing strategy

Following the mixed financing strategy, the GP raises an amount $2K < 2I$ in T_0. In each period, in which he comes across an investment opportunity, the GP is only allowed to spend an amount K from the fund's ex ante capital, forcing him to raise an additional amount $I - K$ each period in order to finance the transaction. The GP issues $w_{P,i}(x_i)$, backed by the respective investment's cash flow in period i, for ex post investors and $w_I(x)$, backed by the fund cash flow, for ex ante investors. The remainder $w_{GP}(x) = x - w_I(x)$ with $x = x_1 - w_{P,1}(x_1) + x_2 - w_{P,2}(x_2)$ represents the GP security. The fly-by-night condition in this case is given by:

Fly-by-night condition:

$$w_{GP}(x) = 0 \; if \; x \leq 2K \qquad (11)$$

According to the setting described, both an optimal ex post and ex ante security is derived subsequently.

Ex post security   As described before, the GP has to raise ex post capital in order to being able to invest into a firm in either of the two periods. In T_1 the issued security $w_{P,1}(x_1)$ has to satisfy the following conditions:

Fly-by-night condition:

---

[52] Based on Axelson, et al. (2009), p. 1563.

$$w_{P,1}(I) - (I - K) \geq 0 \qquad (12)$$

Break-even condition in T_1:

$$w_{P,1}(Z) \geq I - K \qquad (13)$$

The fly-by-night condition prevents fly-by-night operators to raise capital from outside investors, invest at the risk free rate and make a positive profit. The break-even condition ensures that ex post investors receive a minimum payoff of at least $I - K$, if an investment was successful.[53] Meeting both of the two conditions, debt with a face value $F = I - K$, is an optimal ex post security for period 1. If an investment was made in T_1, fly-by-night operators are sorted out and the investor can be sure that there will only be investments in good firms in T_2. Thus, similarly to T_1, the optimal security in period 2 is debt with a face value $F = I - K$. However, if no investment has been made in T_1, the GP has an incentive to invest into any firm he encounters in T_2, since he would receive nothing otherwise. The ex post investor is aware of this situation and consequently poses higher requirements on his break-even condition. The fly-by-night condition stays unchanged.

Break-even condition in T_2:

$$(\alpha + (1 - \alpha)p)w_{P,1}(Z) \geq I - K \qquad (14)$$

The cheapest security for ex post financing in T_2 if no investment has been made in the first period is again debt, but with a higher face value of $F = \frac{I-K}{\alpha+(1-\alpha)p}$. An adaption of the break even condition makes sure that the GP is able to raise capital in the high state and is prevented from investing in the low state:

$$(\alpha_h + (1 - \alpha_h)p)Z \geq I - K \geq (\alpha_L + (1 - \alpha_L)p)Z \qquad (15)$$

If there is no investment in T_1 and a low state in T_2, the investors will not provide ex post financing and thus prevent the GP from investing.

Ex ante security The derivation of an optimal design for both $w_I(x)$ and $w_{GP}(x) = x - w_I(x)$ is similar to the pure ex ante financing case except for two crucial differences. First, the GP only raises $2K < 2I$ ex ante capital and is thus forced to raise additional capital to finance his investments. Second, in situations in which there is only one successful investment, expected cash flows in this case are different from the pure ex ante financing case. With pure ex ante financing it is $E(x) = Z$, independently from whether the good investment occurred in T_1 or T_2. Now, since the ex ante security in the combined financing case is indirectly tied to the payoff of ex post investors, this is different. As described earlier, ex post investors provide capital at a different face value, depending on whether or not there has been an investment in period 1. This effect needs to be incorporated into the ex ante security design.

---

[53] According to the postulated equilibrium there will only be investments into good firms in T_1.

Again, the equilibrium is implemented by solving for $w_{GP}(x)$ under consideration of monotonicity, fly-by-night, break-even and incentive compatibility condition. Additionally it needs to be accounted for the ex ante capital requirement as given by (15). The first three conditions remain the same as in the pure ex ante financing case, while incentive compatibility needs to be adapted according to the different face values of the ex post security.

Incentive compatibility condition with mixed financing:

$$q(\alpha_H + (1-\alpha_H)p)w_{GP}(Z - \frac{I-K}{\alpha_H + (1-\alpha_H)p} + K) \geq \quad (16)$$

$$p(E(\alpha)w_{GP}\big(2(Z-(I-K))\big) + (1-E(\alpha))w_{GP}(Z-(I-K)+K))$$

Condition (16) ensures that the GP does not invest into a bad firm in T_1. Note that this condition also implies that he passes up bad firms in T_2 if he has invested in any firm in the first period. Under the condition that K is set maximal at $K^* = I - (\alpha_L + (1-\alpha_L)p)Z$, the solution to the maximization problem suggests

$$w_I(x) = \min(x, F) + k(\max(x - S, 0)), \quad (17)$$

where $2K^* \leq F \leq S \leq Z - (I - K^*) + K^*$ and $k \in (0, 1]$,

to be an optimal design for the ex ante security. Similarly to the pure ex ante case, the LPs receive their initial investment F plus a share of the cash flows above a threshold S. While the equity component in the ex ante contract is reducing the share of the GP's payoffs and thus mitigates his risk-shifting incentives, the debt component has the effect of screening out fly-by-night operators.

The postulated equilibrium is only stable if ex post and ex ante financing is raised from different parties. If the GP would be required to raise ex post capital from ex ante investors, ex post financing decisions would affect payoffs from ex ante capital and thus lead to inefficient behavior of the LP. In some cases he then would have an incentive to refuse financing even in the high state in T_2 if there was no investment in T_1.[54] Then, however, the GP would not have an incentive to pass up bad firms in T_1 and the equilibrium breaks down. Two important points arise from this argument. First, it is inefficient if ex post financing decisions affect ex ante financing returns. Second, in some cases ex ante investors need to subsidize ex post investors even in the high state in order to facilitate their funding decision. This is especially the case if there has been no investment in the first period. Both requirements can only be met if ex post and ex ante investors are two different parties.

Implications of the model

The model gives an explanation why most private equity transactions are financed with both ex ante equity and ex post debt capital. While equity is giving the GP a certain degree of flexibility in his investment decisions, debt has a certain control function as its availability depends on current capital markets and thus on the current state of the economy as such.

---

[54] This would be the case if $(\alpha_H + (1-\alpha_H)p)Z < I$.

Concerning overall private equity activity, the dependency on ex post financing suggests that if debt is cheap, private equity activity should increase. Additionally, due to the fact that in equilibrium there is underinvestment in the low and overinvestment in the high state, the private equity industry can be expected to amplify natural industry cycles. This observation is also confirmed by recent empirical research.[55]

Regarding the fund structure, the model proposes a restriction on the fraction of equity to be invested each period. This can also be observed in covenants being a common component in LPAs.[56] With respect to the model, in fact the proposed equilibrium would break down if this restriction did not exist as it gave the GP the option to invest $2K$ in one period, making ex post capital obsolete and thus jeopardizing its controlling effect.

The model also gives justification for common practices in GP compensation, suggesting a nonlinear compensation pattern for LPs and a carry catch-up region for GPs before profits are split between the two parties.[57] Consequently, as depicted in Figure 8, the GP is facing a classical asset substitution problem as pointed out by Jensen / Meckling (1976).[58] Due to the debt-like payoff structure of the LP security and the fact, that the GP holds an option-like stake in the fund, which only pays off if $x > 2I$, the fund manager will always have the incentive to invest in riskier projects if fund cash flows are not higher than $2I$. Thus, he is investing his low-risk assets in high-risk investments and therefore transfers value from investors to himself (Figure 8).

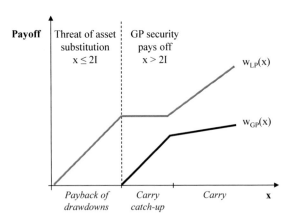

Figure 8: Payoff structure of GP and LP securities[59]

---

[55] See Kaplan / Strömberg (2009), p. 138.
[56] See Gompers / Lerner (1996), p. 478.
[57] See Metrick / Yasuda (2010), p. 11.
[58] See Jensen / Meckling (1976), p. 315.
[59] Modified, based on Axelson, et al. (2009), p. 1560.

More intuitively, this problem can be regarded as a fund manager's behavior in distressed situations. Especially if the GP has consecutively encountered bad firms, which may be indicated by low fund performance or a comparatively low amount of capital invested, he has an increased incentive to overinvest. This higher willingness to take risk may result not only in an increased number of potentially value destroying investments, but also in higher prices a fund manager is willing to pay for prospective targets. According to Axelson, et al. (2009), debt capital providers expect that behavior and demand for a higher face value for their investment. Consequently, debt financing becomes more expensive, which may result in a larger amount of equity used to finance the transaction. The authors further argue that these implications are likely to have a stronger effect on less reputable private equity companies because they much more depend on the current fund's performance than more reputable players. Both ideas are of theoretical nature and have not been empirically observed so far. This study finds empirical evidence for the first and rejects the latter argument in chapter 6.

3.2 Determinants beyond the Principal Agent Conflict

The previous chapter explained potential motivations behind investment structuring decisions in leveraged buyouts. Yet it only focused on a principal agent point of view. Apparently, there might also be other factors that influence these decisions and thus affect both the respective debt and pricing level. The next paragraphs will discuss the most prevailing ones.

3.2.1 Debt Market Conditions

Fund managers need to raise a large amount of money from both equity and debt capital markets in order to fund investments into LBO candidates. As described, the largest part of fund capital is comprised of debt which needs to be raised from banks or other institutional lenders. Hence, it seems natural that the ability of the GP to raise capital for his fund or a specific investment should at least partly depend on the overall economic conditions of the debt market. Under hot credit markets, when cheap loans are available, the PE firm should be able to raise more debt for the same cost as it would be the case under tight credit conditions. Empirical research confirms this assumption and finds that GPs actually do lever their deals higher if LBO spreads are low. In other words, fund managers generally take advantage of favorable credit market conditions and use more debt to finance their transactions when it is cheap.[60] With regard to pricing, evidence can be found for higher prices in leveraged buyout deals during favorable credit market conditions. The authors conclude that the higher transaction prices reflect the fact that GPs are able to finance the price premium with additional debt.[61]

---

[60] See Axelson, et al. (2010), p. 26.
[61] See Axelson, et al. (2010), p. 29.

3.2.2 Reputation of the Private Equity Firm

The reputation of a private equity firm is considered as another characteristic that is important for deal structuring. Especially with regard to fund raising, a rational creditor will always avoid working together with firms that engage in extensive risk-shifting or randomly walk away from deals gone sour.[62] Being mentioned not only by Axelson, et al. (2009) but also by other authors[63] as a potentially important factor in transaction structuring, there is a growing number of empirical research trying to capture reputation effects in the LBO context.

Both Ivashina / Kovner (2008) and Demiroglu / James (2010) examine the impact of a PE firm's reputation on the financing structure of leveraged buyouts. While Ivashina / Kovner (2008) are investigating the impact on loan terms resulting from repeated interactions between the PE sponsor and lending banks, Demiroglu / James (2010) focus on independent reputation measures and their effect on the deal structure per se.

Ivashina / Kovner (2008) identify two potential reasons for banks to grant favorable loan terms to certain PE sponsors. First, through the repeated interaction between PE firm and lead bank, the lender receives private information about the PE firm's processes, compensation structure and risk attitude. The resulting decrease of information asymmetry between the two parties reduces the cost of bank monitoring and screening for future transactions and potentially translates into cheaper debt. Second, the prospects of future fees through financial advisory or other services may also influence debt pricing and structuring. If banks get to advice the exit of a private equity investment, they might be more willing to lend debt at more favorable conditions.[64] The authors find evidence for both of the two arguments described above. Decreased information asymmetry as well as prospective follow-up projects result in lower interest rates and looser financial covenants for the benefit of the private equity sponsor and the portfolio company respectively. This implies that private equity investors serve as an enabler for buyout targets to have access to debt financing at much better conditions than they would have received as a stand-alone company without the support of a PE firm.[65] However, the question whether or not a PE firm's reputation influences its financing decisions is not directly answered in Ivashina / Kovner (2008). In their empirical analysis Demiroglu / James (2010) address this issue.

Demiroglu / James (2010) define reputation of a private equity firm not by its number of interactions with lending banks but develop reputation measures relying on number and volume of a firm's buyout deals over the last three years. Similarly to Ivashina / Kovner (2008), they find that reputable private equity companies pay lower interest rates and receive less stringent covenants.[66] Interestingly, they also look at leverage and transaction pricing

---

[62] Jensen (1989), p. 70.
[63] See Axelson, et al. (2009), p. 1572; Chung, et al. (2010), p. 3; Ljungqvist, et al. (2008), pp. 23f.
[64] See Ivashina / Kovner (2008), p. 2.
[65] See Ivashina / Kovner (2008), p. 1.
[66] See Demiroglu / James (2010), p. 322; The authors find that reputable PE firms have longer maturities on their loans. Short term loans are regarded as a substitute for financial covenants as they imply stricter and more frequent monitoring. Consequently, a longer maturity is a sign for less monitoring requirements and looser covenants.

with respect to the PE firm's reputation. It is found that in leveraged buyouts, reputable PE sponsors use more debt than non-reputable sponsors but do not pay a higher price for the respective target.[67] This is interesting as it means that even though reputable firms profit from cheaper debt, they do not transfer these benefits to the target's shareholders but use it to increase the expected return for their equity investors instead.

Overall, according to recent literature, it can be found that reputable private equity firms benefit from lower interest rates and looser covenants on their loans. There is also some evidence that these benefits translate into higher leverage in buyout transactions. Yet it is not found that reputable PE sponsors pay higher prices as a result of their better access to debt financing. However, due to the limited amount of empirical research available, it still remains to be answered, which variables serve best to approximate PE firm reputation.

3.2.3 Other Determinants of Leverage and Pricing

Besides the LBO specific determinants above, potential factors influencing transaction structuring in leveraged buyouts can also be found in traditional capital structure literature.

Leverage Effect In their 1958 seminal paper, Franco Modigliani and Merton H. Miller developed a model for the cost of capital which fundamentally impacted future corporate finance research. Several authors developed their findings on the basis of the work of Modigliani / Miller and their correction of 1963. Under strict assumptions, the authors showed that the market value of a firm is independent of the respective company's capital structure.[68] They further showed that the required return on equity is increasing with a company's debt ratio.[69] The underlying implications for leveraged buyouts can help to describe a fund manager's incentive to lever a deal. If a GP can boost the return on equity by increasing the amount of debt financing, he will always try to lever his deals as much as possible in order to exploit the pure leverage effect.[70]

Taxes Capital structure theories based on tax advantages have played an important role in explaining a firm's financing choices ever since Modigliani and Miller published their work in 1958 and 1963.[71] The general idea is that the higher the leverage of a company, the higher the associated tax savings due to the deductibility of interest expenses. Through the 1970's, the most prevalent opinion was that the optimal capital structure is a result of a balance between tax advantages and the net present value of bankruptcy cost associated with a higher debt burden. Mainly triggered by Miller (1977), many researchers elaborated on that idea and arrived at a broader definition of the so-called trade-off theory. Accordingly, the capital structure is the result of tax advantages offset by financial distress cost, which include both

---

[67] See Demiroglu / James (2010), p. 325.
[68] See Modigliani / Miller (1958), p. 268.
[69] See Modigliani / Miller (1958), p. 271.
[70] See Axelson, et al. (2010), p. 14.
[71] See Modigliani / Miller (1958) and Modigliani / Miller (1963).

bankruptcy but also all other debt-related cost.[72] Indeed, the corporate tax rate is the only company specific variable for which Axelson, et al. (2010) find a similarity between capital structure decisions in public firms and leveraged buyout financing. Finding this, they confirm earlier research which identifies tax advantages as an important source of value in buyout transactions.[73]

Industry   Titman (1984) regards debt as a tool to commit shareholders to an optimal liquidation point. He arrives at the result that companies producing highly unique products or services can be expected to have less debt than companies acting in a stable industry sector, which is rarely subject to disruptive innovations.[74] In this context, it is further argued that debt levels decrease with the importance of having a reputation for delivering high-quality products.[75] The importance of these industry characteristics can be observed in the selection of leveraged buyout targets, but may also allow conclusions on the use of leverage in actual buyout transactions across different industries. Banks may be willing to accept higher leverage for targets acting in stable industries, which are less sensitive to external effects such as the industrial goods sector. Accordingly, transactions involving portfolio companies, which are active in a more dynamic environment such as the high-tech sector can be expected to be financed with comparably less debt.

Firm Size   Roden / Lewellen (1995) describe three different reasons for larger targets to be financed with a greater portion of debt. First, due to a higher degree of diversification, they have a lower risk of bankruptcy and can expect a more flexible enforcement of a single creditor's claim in case the company does not meet debt service obligations. Second, bankruptcy costs are likely to be lower compared to the total residual value in case of default. Further, they usually hold more sellable assets at their disposal than smaller firms. The proceeds then can be used to meet outstanding obligations. Third, large firms have better access to both debt and equity capital market which increases the number of refinancing options.[76] Overall, transactions involving larger buyout targets can be expected to be financed with a higher amount of debt than it would be the case for smaller firms. Axelson, et al. (2010) show empirically that larger LBO deals are financed with significantly more debt than smaller deals.[77]

---

[72] See Leland (1994), p. 1213.
[73] See Kaplan (1989), p. 630.
[74] See Titman (1984), p. 139.
[75] See Maksimovic / Titman (1991), p. 194.
[76] See Roden / Lewellen (1995), p. 77.
[77] See Axelson, et al. (2010), p. 29.

4 Fund State and Investment Pressure

As previously discussed, it is especially principal agent driven factors, which play an important role in the fund manager's transaction structuring decisions. However, in order to have a certain decision-making basis, there is a necessity for different measures, supporting the GP in assessing the fund's current state. In that context, this chapter introduces commonly used measures and discusses potential dynamics in a fund manager's investment behavior. In the last part of the chapter, three hypotheses are formulated, which are empirically tested in chapter 6.

4.1 Fund Performance

Throughout relevant literature, internal rate of return (IRR) is the predominant measure for PE fund performance.[78] In contrast to a standard NPV calculation, which finds the NPV of an investment given a specified discount rate, the IRR method finds the respective discount rate given a NPV of zero. Consequently, an investment or a buyout transaction is value enhancing for investors, if the actual cost of capital are below the calculated IRR. In contrast, if the investment's cost of capital are higher, it is value destroying. Fund level performance is measured similarly by using fund cash flows across all investments conducted.[79] Poor fund performance can have various sources and may be caused by both internal and external factors. A GP, who selects bad targets and does a poor job in increasing operational efficiency in his portfolio companies, is possibly facing lower fund performance than fund managers with better skills. Externally, fund performance may be also negatively influenced by bad capital market conditions or a limited availability of good investment opportunities, e.g. through increased competition among PE companies.

Kaplan / Schoar (2005) find that fund performance increases with both the GP's skills and size of the fund for buyouts between 1980 and 2001. They further find that fund performance is lower in boom markets characterized by a high number of new funds raised and limited availability of good investment opportunities.[80] These findings remain to be persistent, yet weaker, when the time horizon is extended until 2010 and thus includes buyouts, which were conducted during the competitive buyout period in the mid 2000's.[81]

While IRR strongly depends on the timing of cash flows and is thus harder to predict, fund managers often use money multiples (also: cash-on-cash multiple) in order to approximate an investment's performance. The money multiple is defined as the amount of cash a GP receives from an investment divided by the amount initially invested into the target compa-

---

[78] See Achleitner, et al. (2011), p. 1; Kaplan / Schoar (2005), p. 1797; Robinson / Sensoy (2010), p. 6.
[79] See Pindur (2007), p. 61.
[80] See Kaplan / Schoar (2005), p. 1821.
[81] See Robinson / Sensoy (2010), p. 34.

ny.⁸² As it can be calculated quickly and represents an investor's success more directly, money multiple is a very common measure in the private equity space. Since throughout the analysis in chapter 6, the GP is assumed to have a certain understanding of the overall fund performance rather than to predict monthly cash flows, this study relies on money multiples as performance measure.

4.2 Capital Invested

Another important measure is the capital invested (CI) ratio of a private equity fund. Total capital invested represents the amount of capital which was drawn down from equity investors and directly invested into portfolio companies.⁸³ The CI ratio, as the amount of capital invested in relation to total committed capital, thus indicates how heavily a buyout fund has been investing. In their analysis, Ljungqvist, et al. (2008) find three major factors determining the amount of capital invested in buyout funds. First, higher overall quality of investment opportunities has a positive effect on capital invested. Second, if bargaining power increases and buyout funds find themselves in situations with only little competition, they invest more heavily. Third, capital invested increases under favorable credit conditions. Thus, consistently with the findings of Axelson, et al. (2010), if debt is cheap, PE firms invest more often.⁸⁴

4.3 Investment Pressure and Hypotheses

Since CI ratio and performance describe the current state of a PE fund, they are important for both internal and external stakeholders of a private equity firm. Thus, different levels of these measures may cause a certain degree of investment pressure for the respective fund manager. In the theoretical literature, this pressure is mostly a result of the principal agent conflict the GP is engaged in. Besides Axelson, et al. (2009), whose model was already introduced in detail, especially Ljungqvist, et al. (2008) and Chung, et al. (2010) contributed to the research on the investment behavior of private equity funds. These works should serve as a supplement to the model of Axelson, et al. (2009) and set the main ground for the development of different hypotheses which are empirically tested in the subsequent chapters.

Ljungqvist, et al. (2008) analyze the investment behavior of buyout funds and find that fund managers reduce the risk in the second half of their lives when they have achieved more exits or returned more capital to their investors in the first half.⁸⁵ This behavior is similar to the one developed by the equilibrium strategy of Axelson, et al. (2009), which states that GPs, who have already invested in an early period, will invest less often in subsequent periods.⁸⁶ In other words, both models suggest the GP to invest more actively and less risk-averse in later periods if only a few investments have been made in earlier periods. In these situations, GPs

---

⁸² See Pindur (2007), p. 60.
⁸³ See Pindur (2007); p. 53.
⁸⁴ See Ljungqvist, et al. (2008), pp. 26f.
⁸⁵ See Ljungqvist, et al. (2008), p. 25.
⁸⁶ See Axelson, et al. (2009), p. 1563.

obviously face a certain investment pressure which guides them into an investment behavior they would not follow in a less distressed situation. Axelson, et al. (2009) relates that behavior to the convex return structure of GP compensation.[87] If there have not been any successful investments in the beginning of the fund lifecycle, fund managers are likely to invest into riskier deals in subsequent periods. On the one hand, this behavior maximizes the expected return for fund managers, but on the other hand, it also increases risk for debt holders. Similar to the classical asset substitution problem,[88] debt providers know about this behavior and thus react with higher borrowing costs or a limitation of the lending capacity.[89] This might lead to a situation where fund managers are under pressure to do deals, but, while being willing to pay a higher price to increase a deal's likelihood, have difficulties to obtain adequate debt financing from banks. In this setting, ex ante investors (i.e. equity providers) need to subsidize the transaction so that the deal can take place.[90] To confirm these theoretical findings empirically, the following hypothesis has to hold:

Hypothesis 1 (H1)   *A low capital invested ratio should result in lower leverage as well as in an increased willingness to pay higher prices.*

Moving on, the second hypothesis focuses on how fund performance measures influence a fund manager's investment behavior. Even though a large part of the literature emphasizes the importance of a GP's direct compensation from the fund's cash flows,[91] it rarely happens that a fund manager only raises one fund in his career. Usually GPs raise one fund after another, a fact that should also find consideration when examining investment behavior. Chung, et al. (2010) investigate the importance of explicit as opposed to implicit compensation and find that implicit compensation, arising from the GPs prospect to raise follow-on funds, contributes substantially to the overall incentive structure. In addition they find that probability and size of a follow-on fund are significantly related to the performance of earlier funds of the fund manager.[92] Hence, accounting for multiple fund raisings throughout the GP's career increases his dependency on the current fund's performance and thus may lead to investment pressure similar to the one described by Axelson, et al. (2009). If fund managers are facing poor fund performance compared to other buyout funds, they are forced to boost their own fund's performance in order to being able to raise the next generation fund.[93] This may increase their willingness to do marginal deals for which they pay higher prices.[94] At the same time, the implications on leverage may be twofold. One option is that leverage increases as a result of the GP's willingness to take higher risk and to boost return on equity.[95] This option implies that the fund manager takes advantage of the pure leverage effect as described by

---

[87] See Figure 8, p. 23.
[88] See Jensen / Meckling (1976), p. 315.
[89] See Axelson, et al. (2009), p. 1566.
[90] See Axelson, et al. (2010), p. 14.
[91] See Metrick / Yasuda (2010), p. 2304 and Gompers / Lerner (1999), p. 4.
[92] See Chung, et al. (2010), pp. 3f.
[93] See Chung, et al. (2010), p. 8.
[94] See Axelson, et al. (2009), p. 1572.
[95] See Kaplan / Stein (1993), p. 355; The authors identify the easy access to debt as a potential reason for the crash in the junk bond market in the late 80's. Fund managers took riskier deals with higher leverage in order to achieve excess returns.

Modigliani / Miller (1958),[96] but requires the GP to have the power to independently decide how much debt to raise for the individual transaction. The second option is a decrease in leverage, taking into account that an independent decision on the debt level is not readily possible as debt providers are aware of the asset substitution problem and limit their lending capacities to poor performing funds due to GP's incentive to do riskier investments.[97] Both ideas are incorporated into the second hypothesis.

Hypothesis 2 (H2) *Low fund performance should result in an increased willingness to pay higher prices and*

> *a) in higher leverage, due to an increased willingness of fund managers to take higher risk and their power to independently decide upon respective leverage levels, or*
>
> *b) in lower leverage, due to the debt providers' awareness of the asset substitution problem and the associated limitation of lending capacities for poor performing funds.*

Both Axelson, et al. (2009), Chung, et al. (2010) and Ljungqvist, et al. (2008) suggest, that the in H1 and H2 described effects of investment pressure can be expected to be stronger for younger, less reputable private equity firms. These firms are lacking an extensive track record and thus are more sensitive to performance and CI effects.[98] Having already demonstrated to be able to manage successful funds, older PE firms can bear failure much better than younger firms, which still need to prove their ability of being a successful PE investor.[99] This amplifying effect of a low reputation is formalized in the third hypothesis:

Hypothesis 3 (H3) *The effects of H1 and H2 should be stronger for GPs with low reputation.*

In order to test the three hypotheses described above, the dataset, on which the analysis is based on, is introduced in chapter 5. Results of the empirical analysis are described in chapter 6.

---

[96] See Modigliani / Miller (1958), p. 271.
[97] See Axelson, et al. (2009), p. 1566.
[98] See Axelson, et al. (2009), p. 1572; Chung, et al. (2010), p. 3; Ljungqvist, et al. (2008), pp. 23f.
[99] See Gompers / Lerner (1996), p. 466; The authors show that especially younger venture capital firms tend to take portfolio companies public prematurely in order to establish a track record more quickly.

5 Data Description

The investigated subsample is formed from an extensive dataset of 11,177 buyout transactions between 1985 and 2009, collected by two European funds-of-funds in the course of their due diligence efforts. Besides information on the associated PE sponsor and the respective fund, there is also detailed transaction and target company data available. Missing data on fund manager foundation year, number of deals per year and fund size was derived from the Thomson Reuters Private Equity database.

On transaction level, besides general company information and deal characteristics, the dataset contains extensive financial data. Specifically, for a large number of transactions there is full information on monthly gross cash flows,[100] which are exchanged between target and PE firm through the course of the investment period. Further, the dataset contains enterprise value (EV), net debt, equity value, EBITDA as well as sales data for both the entry and exit of the transaction. All financial figures have been converted into Euro, using the respective exchange rate at the time. In order to being able to control for industry specifics, each buyout target in the subsample was manually reviewed and classified according to the first level Industry Classification Benchmark (ICB)[101]. Data on economic indicators as well as industry specific financial measures were obtained from Thomson Reuters Datastream as well as the research section of the Federal Reserve (Board of Governors of the Federal Reserve System)[102].

Fund performance and CI variables were calculated on the basis of the whole dataset of 11,177 transactions, while the subsample was derived in order to analyze the fund managers' investment behavior. The following selection criteria were applied for the construction of the subsample: First, capital structure data for the entry date of the respective transaction was available. Second, the entry date was at least three years after the fund's vintage year in order to ensure the availability of appropriate fund performance data. Third, the transaction has at least one fund performance variable without unrealized deal impact. Unrealized deals are transactions, (i) which have not been sold during the reporting period or (ii) where only limited financial information on the sale is available. Since these transactions distort the whole fund performance variable, only variables, which are calculated exclusively on the basis of realized deals, are taken into account.

---

[100] Gross of fees and carry.
[101] See Dow Jones Indexes (2011).
[102] See Board of Governors of the Federal Reserve System (2011).

5.1 Sample Characteristics and Representativeness

Subsample The restrictions described above reduced the initial dataset to a subsample of 1,190 transactions with a total value of more than €530bn. Descriptive statistics regarding geographical and industry distribution are given in Panel A of Table 3. 754 (63%) of the buyouts analyzed are from Europe, 423 (36%) from North America and 13 (1%) from the rest of the world. Compared to the whole LBO universe, this distribution is slightly underweighting North American and overweighting European as well as Rest of World buyouts.[103] However, this shift is not as substantial as it can be expected to adversely affect the results and the dataset can still be considered as representative with respect to geographical distribution. Particularly regarding the distribution of investments among different industries, the subsample can be considered as a good proxy for the LBO universe. A large number of the buyout targets in the sample come from the Industrial, Consumer Services or Consumer Goods industry. This is comparable with overall buyout activity as depicted in Panel B of Table 3.

Panel A: Geographical Distribution				Panel B: Buyouts per Industry			
Region	Number of Investments	Percentage	LBO Universe*	Industry	Number of Investments	Percentage	LBO Universe*
Europe	754	63%	47%	Industrials	371	32%	26%
North America	423	36%	47%	Consumer Services	289	25%	21%
Rest of World	13	1%	6%	Consumer Goods	162	14%	13%
Total	*1190*	*100%*		Technology	105	9%	6%
				Health Care	87	7%	6%
				Financials	55	5%	5%
				Telecommunications	45	4%	6%
				Basic Materials	36	3%	8%
				Oil & Gas	11	1%	1%
				Utilities	9	1%	2%
* Data derived from Strömberg (2007)				*Total*	*1170*	*100%*	

Table 3: Summary statistics of dataset[104]

As depicted in Table 4, the average enterprise value across the sample is €446m and the median €102m. Both values are higher than those identified by Strömberg (2007),[105] indicating that the investigated sample has a slight bias towards larger deals. The average gearing ratio (net debt divided by equity value) is 2.64. This translates into a debt ratio (net debt divided by enterprise value) of approximately 73%. In other words, on average, more than two thirds of the enterprise value is financed with outside debt. This number is in line with the findings of Axelson, et al. (2010), who identify 69% as an average debt ratio in their sample.[106]

---

[103] See Strömberg (2007), p. 31.
[104] Own source. A reference table for the industries identified by Strömberg (2007) can be found in the Appendix.
[105] See Strömberg (2007), p. 33; The author finds an average (median) enterprise value of $318m ($61m).
[106] See Axelson, et al. (2010), p. 20.

	N	min	p25	p50	mean	p75	max	sd
EV (€m)	1190	1	33	102	446	345	11,969	1,045
Debt (€m)	1130	(45)	17	57	287	229	8,024	714
Equity (€m)	1190	0	12	42	174	134	5,731	442
Debt / Equity	1130	0.0	0.9	1.6	2.6	2.5	40.7	5.0
Debt / EBITDA	1065	(5.7)	2.8	3.9	4.9	5.3	49.1	6.5

Table 4: Transaction financials at entry[107]

It is worth noting that similar to the findings of Axelson, et al. (2010), debt and valuation levels increased in the late 90's, decreased in the course of the new economy bubble in the early 20's and increased again in the period thereafter (Figure 9).[108] Statistics on a yearly basis also reveal that EV / EBITDA and Net Debt / EBITDA are closely following each other over the years.[109]

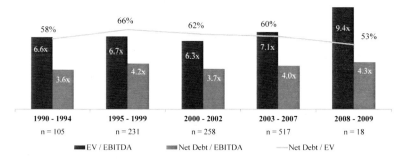

Figure 9: EBITDA multiple, debt ratio and debt / EBITDA over time[110]

With regard to investment performance, during an average holding period of 4.11 years, the median equity IRR amounted to 30% and the median money multiple to 2.2x (Table 5).[111] These numbers are only slightly higher than those reported by Lopez de Silanes, et al. (2009), who investigated a large and representative sample of 5,106 realized transactions and find a median of 26% and 2.1x respectively.[112]

---

[107] Own source.
[108] See Axelson, et al. (2010), p. 42.
[109] See Appendix 2.
[110] Own source; Time categories adapted from Strömberg (2007), p. 33; Period of 1985 – 1989 intentionally left out due do the low number of observations.
[111] Note that these performance measures are derived on the basis of cash flows gross of fees and carry.
[112] See Lopez de Silanes, et al. (2009), p. 46.

	N	min	p25	p50	mean	p75	max	sd
Money Multiple	1190	0.0	1.2	2.2	3.0	3.6	165.3	5.7
IRR	1135	-100%	7%	30%	43%	64%	392%	70%
Holding Period	840	0.0	2.4	3.5	4.1	5.1	17.8	2.6

Table 5: Investment performance statistics[113]

Fund Performance & Capital Invested   As mentioned, fund performance and CI variables were calculated on the basis of all transactions in the extensive database of 11,177 LBOs, for which respective financial information was available. This approach is necessary, since it cannot be ensured that all transactions of a specific fund are part of the subsample.

The whole database comprises transactions from 722 different buyout funds with an average (median) fund size of €1.1bn (€0.4bn). Figure 10 depicts the median money multiple of all funds in the dataset on the basis of gross cash flows from all realized fund investments until a certain time in the fund's lifecycle. The variables were calculated by dividing the accumulated positive by the accumulated negative gross cash flows of deals exited until the respective year after fund initiation. Note that for the reasons described above, these statistics specifically exclude fund performance measures which are partly based on financial information of unrealized deals. Funds in year five after initiation[114] have a median money multiple of 2.1x. Naturally, this number is increasing with fund age when additional profitable investments are made. Still, the five year money multiple is considerably higher than the one reported by Kaplan / Schoar (2005), who find a median money multiple of 1.5x for a sample of 336 buyout funds between 1980 and 2001.[115] This difference is due to the fact that the performance measured by Kaplan / Schoar is net of management fee and carry and thus underestimating the funds' actual performance.[116] After a fund age of ten years, money multiples are not significantly increasing as usually the limited partnership ends after this period of time and no additional investments are made. However, funds may still sell off existing investments, which explains the comparably high number of observations until year 15.[117]

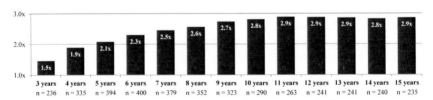

Figure 10: Median money multiple by fund age in years[118]

---

[113] Own source.
[114] In this analysis, the year of fund initiation is equivalent to the fund's vintage year.
[115] See Kaplan / Schoar (2005), p. 1800.
[116] See Kaplan / Schoar (2005), p. 1791.
[117] See Ljungqvist, et al. (2008), p. 36.
[118] Own source; The number of observations is lower than total number of funds in the dataset. This is due to two reasons: Firstly, as soon as a fund performance measure is partly based on unrealized deals, it is exclud-

The CI variable was calculated by dividing the accumulated fund investments (i.e. the negative cash flows), made until a certain point of time in the fund lifecycle, by the total fund size. The median CI ratio for a five year old fund is 83%. Again, CI is increasing with fund age and reaches a median of 98% for funds in year ten, with more than a third (33.8%) of all funds having drawn down and invested the full amount of committed capital.[119]

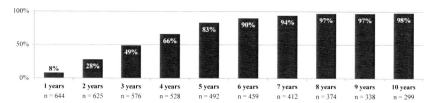

Figure 11: Median capital invested ratio by fund age in years[120]

Overall, the sample used in this study can be regarded as representative. It replicates both regional and industry distribution of all buyout transactions during the period between 1985 and 2009. Financial measures on transaction and fund level are in line with other empirical research such as the work from Axelson, et al. (2010), Lopez de Silanes, et al. (2009) and Strömberg (2007). Additionally, the dataset includes all transactions, even if the data-providing funds-of-funds did eventually not invest into the respective fund. Thus, a bias towards more successful funds can be ruled out. Performance and CI measures are based on a comprehensive dataset of 11,177, covering a large part of the overall buyout universe during the period of 1985 and 2009. Moreover, performance variables are not subject to a self-reporting bias since they are derived directly from cash flows reported by the respective private equity firm in the course of their fundraising activity. Altogether, performance and CI variables as well as the investigated subsample represent the LBO universe to a good degree and an independent composition of the sample can be confidently claimed.

---

ed from the calculation. For 415 funds, the fund performance measure in year three is based on unrealized deals. Secondly, fund could not be calculated as there was either no cash flow information available or the first investment was exited after that year. This applied to 71 funds in year three.

[119] See Ljungqvist, et al. (2008), p. 36; Usually the limited partnership lasts ten years and may be extended by a few years contingent on the limited partners' approval.

[120] Own source; The number of observations is lower than the total number of funds in the dataset. This is due to the fact, that the fund size variable was only available for a limited number of funds (654). Additionally, for some of those funds, there was not sufficient transaction data available to calculate the CI ratio (applied to 10 transactions for the first year). The decreasing number of observations can be explained with a fund's last investment being made before year ten.

5.2 Explanatory Variables

In order to determine the impact of investment pressure on transaction structuring decisions, comprehensive variables have to be created, which serve as an indicator for the current state of the fund. In that context, it is relied on both performance and CI measures. The following section describes the composition of these variables as well as how they are transformed to a meaningful investment pressure variable that can be included into the multivariate analysis in chapter 6. Additionally, different reputation measures, which are used as explanatory variables, are introduced.

5.2.1 Fund Performance Variable

Throughout the empirical analysis, the GP is assumed to be able to estimate his investments' performance a certain time into the future. Especially if the holding period is drawing towards the end and all value enhancing measures have been employed, prospective cash flows are more or less predictable with an appropriate certainty. This assumption is based on empirical findings that the major part of all value-creating measures is set in the first 100 days of an investment.[121] As a result, the current fund performance, the GP partly bases his investment decision on, does not only depend on the performance of already sold, but also on soon-to-be sold portfolio companies. This "expected" performance is approximated by the actual fund performance based on future cash flows, which are available for the subsample.

Naturally, capital structure and pricing decisions are made at entry of an investment.[122] For each of those transactions of a fund, two different money multiple variables on fund level have been calculated, accounting for all deals that were at the latest exited one or two years after the investigated transaction.[123] Different from fund performance statistics depicted in Figure 10, not the fund's age but the entry date of the respective transaction served as a reference point for calculation. An illustrative example of this approach is depicted in Figure 12.

---

[121] See Acharya, et al. (2010), p. 35.
[122] See Pindur (2007), p. 34.
[123] As mentioned, it seemed more intuitive to use money multiples instead of IRR measures, since they are not sensitive to cash flow timing. The GP is not assumed to predict monthly cash flows but rather to have an understanding of the overall investment performance. This fact is better covered with future based performance measures on a money multiple basis.

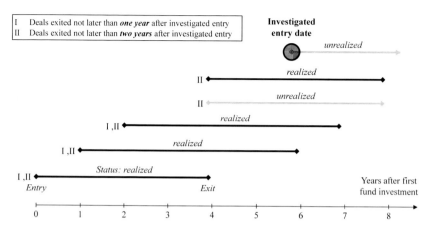

Figure 12: Calculation of performance variables[124]

First, depending on the respective transaction under investigation, performance variables I and II are calculated. The calculation is done on the basis of the accumulated cash flows of all investments of a fund, which were exited within the respective period as given by the definition of the performance variable. In the example, there are cash flows from three investments considered in performance variable I and from five in performance variable II. A GP, who is assumed to predict the overall performance of the fund's investments one year into the future, would thus take into account performance variable I, when deciding on capital structure and pricing of an additional investment. Note that in this example, performance variable II is impacted by unrealized deals and would be excluded from the regression analysis.

Descriptive statistics of these variables are depicted in Table 6.[125] By definition, most both distinct and total observations are made for the performance variable involving all deals exited not later than two years after the entry date of the specific deal. For that variable the average money multiple is 2.8x, which is comparable to the average performance of a five year old fund.[126]

	n	min	p25	p50	mean	p75	max	sd
P-I	929	0.00	1.38	2.15	2.75	3.31	165.34	5.84
P-II	1095	0.00	1.51	2.34	2.78	3.31	46.11	3.12

Table 6: Fund performance variable summary statistics[127]

To account for unrealized deal impact, only money multiples based on cash flows from realized investments are taken into the regression analysis performed in chapter 6 unterhalb.

---
[124] Own source.
[125] Statistics calculated before accounting for unrealized deal impact.
[126] See Appendix 3.
[127] Own source.

5.2.2 Capital Invested Variable

According to Chung, et al. (2010), for the fund manager it is important to know how much capital is already tied up in the portfolio and how much is still at his disposal and may be used to finance additional investments. Consequently, CI ratio is the second measure taken into account when modeling the informative basis for a GP's investment decision. Again, different from the statistics depicted in Figure 11, not the fund's age, but the entry date of the respective transaction was taken as a reference point for the calculation. In order to avoid distortions from including the value of the investigated transaction into the CI calculation, the variable was computed for both one and two years before the entry date of the specific investment. This approach is providing the additional opportunity to assess the fund's capital invested over time before the actual investment was conducted.

Summary statistics are depicted in Table 7. For 1,116 transactions of the subsample it was possible to calculate a capital invested variable for the year before the specific deal was entered, with the average ratio being 38%. By definition, both the number of observations and the average CI ratio is decreasing with a reduction of the time span. Thus, the average CI ratio two years before investment entry is lower at 22%.

	n	min	p25	p50	mean	p75	max	sd
CI-II	*1087*	0.00	0.05	0.17	0.22	0.36	0.89	0.20
CI-I	*1116*	0.00	0.18	0.37	0.38	0.54	0.94	0.22

Table 7: Capital invested variable summary statistics[128]

5.2.3 Investment Pressure Variables

Since it would be wrong to compare performance or CI ratio of a five year old fund with the respective measures of a ten year old fund, it is not possible to simply include the absolute value of these measures into the regression. Thus, in order to analyze a fund manager's investment behavior at entry of a specific transaction, the level of respective fund performance and CI measures needs to be compared to the one of funds in the same phase of their lifecycle. In order to do so, fund statistics calculated across funds of similar age (See Figure 10, Figure 11 and Appendix 3) were used as a reference point in order to determine whether a specific transaction was initiated in a phase of low, medium or high fund performance and CI ratio, respectively. Accordingly, a dummy was created for each performance and CI variable, indicating the level of the respective measure to be either below top quartile, below top third or below median with regard to comparable funds of the whole dataset.

Having determined the level of each performance and CI variable, additional subgroups were created in a second step in order to identify those transactions, which were initiated in situations where the respective variable was consecutively low with regard to the fund manager's time horizon. For example, the two year lowest quartile performance dummy takes

---

[128] Own source.

a value of 1, if the fund performance in year one and two after the entry was located in the lowest quartile. Accordingly, the dummy takes a value of 0 if this was only the case in one or none of the two consecutive years after the transaction was initiated. Hence, these "two years in a row" variables identify funds, which had a sustainable performance or CI level and sorts out those with only temporarily high or low levels. As a consequence, regression results based on these dummies should be more meaningful.

There are 943 transactions in the dataset, whose performance variables with a time horizon of up to two years are not distorted by cash flows from unrealized deals. Out of this, 496 deals (or 52.6%) were initiated in a situation where the fund manager was looking at below top-quartile fund performance for the next two consecutive years. 548 (or 58.1%) deals were initiated by funds whose capital invested has been below median for the last two years in a row. The overlap of these two groups comprises 286 deals. This implies that the slight majority (57.7%) of all below top-quartile performing funds faced a prior period of low capital invested.

5.2.4 Reputation Variables

Reputation of PE firms is measured in various ways across literature.[129] However, most long-term reputation measures can be categorized into three different groups: Value-driven measures, Number-driven measures and Age.[130]

Value-driven measures   Value-driven measures include all reputation variables that are calculated on the basis of monetary investment volumes. Examples are fund size, total assets under management or market share. While an advantage of these measures is the fact that they reflect the firm's success in fundraising and thus the investors' trust in its skills, they suppose that all buyout firms pursue the similar goal of raising and investing as much capital as possible. However, there are indeed private equity firms that specialize in a certain deal size and value-driven measures especially overweight firms focusing on larger deals.[131]

Number-driven measures   Measures from this category are based on the number of interactions PE firms encounter with third parties in a buyout context. An example is the number of loans underwritten by the same bank[132] or the absolute number of transactions. These measures mitigate the problem of overweighting PEs specialized in larger deals but are very sensitive to market-driven effects on a firm's investment activity.

Age   The age of a private equity firm can be assessed by the time that has passed since its foundation or by other measures such as the generation of its latest fund. Both measures indicate that a PE firm has apparently been somehow successful and has been able to survive

---

[129] See Demiroglu / James (2010), p. 318; Gompers (1995), p. 1462; Meuleman, et al. (2009), p. 642.
[130] The categories are adapted from Demiroglu / James (2010), p. 318.
[131] See Demiroglu / James (2010), p. 318.
[132] See Ivashina / Kovner (2008), p. 19.

in the market.[133] However, it neglects the information whether or not the firm has been actively investing and thus was constantly interacting with banks or portfolio companies in order to establish a good reputation.

Due to the fact that each reputation measure has both strengths and weaknesses, this study relies on multiple variables to test whether a firm's long-term reputation impacts a fund manager's investment structuring decision. Thus, to account for reputation effects, the following measures served as primary variables in the subsequent empirical analysis:

1. AUM as the accumulated equity values of all deals which were made within five years prior the entry year of the respective deal[134]
2. Age of the PE firm at the time of entry as the difference between entry year and foundation year
3. Generation of the fund the respective investment is assigned to

In the dataset the median age of a PE firm is 15 years. The median transaction was conducted by a firm with AUMs of €1.1bn, in the third generation fund (Table 8).

	N	min	p25	p50	mean	p75	max	sd
AUM 5y (€bn)	*1096*	0	0.4	1.1	2.3	2.9	16.4	3.1
Age of PE Firm	*1190*	0	8	15	15	20	37	8
Fund Generation	*1189*	0	2	3	3	4	14	2

Table 8: Reputation statistics at entry date[135]

---

[133] See Meuleman, et al. (2009), p. 625.
[134] This is based on the assumption that the average holding period for an investment is five years, which is in line with the value of 4.11 calculated from the dataset.
[135] Own source.

6 Results

In order to test the three hypotheses introduced in chapter 4.3, the different explanatory variables were included into a basic multivariate regression model for leverage and pricing. While the composition of the corresponding explanatory variables will be described in the beginning of each section, the specification of the basic regression remains the same throughout the whole analysis and thus is only introduced once.

It is well documented that there exists an endogeneity between LBO leverage and pricing.[136] In order to account for this fact, both a standard ordinary least squares (OLS) model and an instrumental (IV) regression model with the two stage least square estimator (2sls) were used to conduct the analyses. In the IV 2sls model, LBO spreads as well as the natural logarithm of enterprise value were used as instruments to predict leverage. Even though, both variables have a significant impact on buyout pricing in an OLS regression, it is assumed that these effects come through the leverage channel to the largest extent. In order to gain more comfort with the approach of using an IV 2sls regression model, there are several tests that can be conducted. The Durbin-Wu Hausman test checks for endogeneity of the variables by comparing the results of an OLS and an IV regression. In addition, an F-test of the joint significance of the instruments in the first stage regression can be used to test for weak instruments.[137]

6.1 Basic Regression

Table 9 depicts the results of the basic regression using the OLS and IV 2sls regression model. The dependent variables are leverage (log Net Debt / EBITDA), gearing (log Net Debt / Equity) and multiple (log EV / EBITDA).[138]

In order to rule out both internal and external side-effects, different controlling variables are used throughout the analysis. First, transaction value clearly affects leverage as described in chapter 3.2.3, and the natural logarithm of EV is thus included as a controlling variable. It is also controlled for profitability, using the EBITDA margin at investment entry. Additionally, it is controlled for regional effects, using a dummy variable for each of the three different regions (i.e. Europe, North America, Rest of World). If the deal took place within the respective region, the dummy takes a value of 1 and 0 if not. To control for industry specific characteristics both a dummy variable for the respective industries (i.e. Oil & Gas, Basic Materials, Industrials, Consumer Goods, Health Care, Consumer Services, Telecommunications, Utilities, Financials, Technology) as well as average industry financials are included into the regression. The industry classification was conducted according to first level ICB

---

[136] See Axelson, et al. (2010), p. 63; Demiroglu / James (2010), p. 326.
[137] See Baum (2006), pp. 207ff.
[138] See Axelson, et al. (2010), p. 55; The natural logarithm of these variables is used since it can be assumed that changes on a low level have a greater impact than changes on a high level.

codes. Industry financials were calculated on the basis of second level ICB codes.[139] Furthermore, it is controlled for systematic time effects, using entry year dummies for each transaction. To control for debt market conditions LBO spreads at entry were included, approximated by the yield spread between Moody's BAA seasoned corporate bond yield and 10 year US government bonds at the time of the transaction.

As depicted in Table 9, the number of observations drops from 1,190 to around 800. This decrease mainly comes from transactions with negative leverage, where the natural logarithm could not be applied. Additionally, for a small number of transactions, industry financials were not available. In general, the results confirm many previously discussed effects. The use of debt strongly depends on debt market conditions at entry, with LBO spreads being negatively related to LBO leverage and gearing (1% level).[140] Furthermore, it is found that the larger a target company's enterprise value, the more debt is used by the private equity firm to finance the transaction (1% level). The coefficient for the EBITDA margin is negative, suggesting that more profitable buyout targets are financed with less leverage (10% level for specifications 1 and 3a). This is presumably due to the fact that further margin improvements are more difficult to realize. As to transaction pricing, leverage as well as gearing at investment entry have a strongly positive effect. This indicates that the GP is willing to pay a higher price if he is able to lever up his deal and thus implicitly increases the value of his option-like stake in the buyout fund.[141]

The Durbin-Wu-Hausman test yields a p-value below 1% for both specification (3) and (4), so the hypothesis of leverage and gearing being exogenous can confidently be rejected. In the second step, it was tested for weak instruments looking at the robust F-statistics of the first stage. For (4a) and (5a), F-statistics are 44.13 and 24.24, well above 10 and thus suggesting that the instruments used in the regression are sufficiently strong.[142] Since there is no significant difference between the results of OLS and the first stage IV 2sls, for all following regressions only IV 2sls is reported for both the first and the second stage. Robust F-statistics are always given on the bottom of the regression table. It is further found that the use of gearing and leverage as explanatory variables yield similar results. Thus, for reasons of clarity, only the results of the leverage regressions are reported in the following tables.

---

[139] See Dow Jones Indexes (2011).
[140] See Axelson, et al. (2010), pp. 60f.
[141] See Axelson, et al. (2010), p. 14.
[142] See Stock, et al. (2002), p. 522.

Table 9: Basic Regression Results

The table presents the results of the OLS and the IV2sls regression on the determinants of leverage and pricing of leveraged buyouts using a sample of 1,190 PE sponsored buyouts completed between 1985 and 2009. Log Leverage (Net Debt/EBITDA), log Gearing (Net Debt / Equity) and log Multiple (EV / EBITDA) are the natural logarithms of the respective variable at entry. Log Multiple Industry and log Leverage Industry use figures of public companies in North America (Stoxx Americas 600) and Europe (EURO Stoxx Total Market Index) from Thomson One Banker matched by ICB sector codes and year. They are calculated in the same fashion as the dependent variables. EBITDA Margin is EBITDA divided by Sales at entry. Log Leverage at Entry is the fitted value from the first stage regression on all variables at entry. In the second stage regression as well as the instruments LBO Spreads and the natural logarithm of the Enterprise Value. Finally, region, time and industry dummies are included. Generally, the numbers in the upper rows represent the regression coefficients. *, ** and *** indicate p-values of 10 %, 5% and 1% significance level, respectively. In the lower rows the detailed t-statistics are reported in parentheses.

	OLS			IV2sls			
VARIABLES	log Leverage (1)	log Gearing (2)	log Multiple (3)	log Leverage (4a)	log Gearing (5a)	log Multiple (4b)	log Multiple (5b)
Log Multiple Industry			0.023	-0.047	-0.151	0.094	0.274
			(-0.17)	(-0.23)	(-0.55)	(-0.94)	(-0.92)
EBITDA Margin	-0.153*	0.006	-0.119***	-0.153*	0.001	-0.021	-0.125
	(-1.94)	(-0.07)	(-3.757)	(-1.92)	(0.01)	(-0.55)	(-1.24)
LBO Spreads at Entry	-4.050***	-15.906***	1.736**	-4.106***	-15.875***		
	(-3.36)	(-5.48)	(-2.15)	(-3.28)	(-5.51)		
Log Enterprise Value	0.205***	0.125***	0.150***	0.204***	0.123***		
	(-9.15)	(-4.50)	(-8.19)	(9.01)	(4.45)		
Log Leverage at Entry						0.664***	
						(-11.59)	
Log Leverage Industry	0.081*			0.080*		-0.013	
	(-1.85)			(1.83)		(-0.58)	
Log Gearing at Entry							1.010***
							(-4.24)
Log Gearing Industry		0.139**			0.138**		-0.069
		(-2.25)			(2.23)		(-0.87)
Industries	Yes	Yes	Yes	Yes	Yes	Yes	Yes
Regions	Yes	Yes	Yes	Yes	Yes	Yes	Yes
Time	Yes	Yes	Yes	Yes	Yes	Yes	Yes
Instruments							
LBO Spreads	N/A	N/A	N/A			Yes	Yes
Enterprise Value	N/A	N/A	N/A			Yes	Yes
Constant	7.822***	28.214***	-1.489	6.976***	28.000***	1.710***	2.058*
	(-2.85)	(-5.74)	(-1.00)	(3.07)	(5.63)	(-4.38)	(-1.74)
Observations	824	813	956	823	800	823	800
R-squared	0.17	0.13	0.18	0.17	0.13	0.38	.
F-Statistics	N/A	N/A	N/A	44.13	24.24		

t-statistics in parentheses
*** p<0.01, ** p<0.05, * p<0.1

6.2 Capital Invested Hypothesis

Hypothesis 1 (H1)   *A low capital invested ratio should result in lower leverage as well as in an increased willingness to pay higher prices.*

Table 10 reports the result for IV 2sls regressions using leverage (log EBITDA / Net Debt) and entry multiple (log EV / EBITDA) as dependent and CI dummies as independent variables. All other variables are similar to the specification of the basic regression introduced in the previous section. The difference between specifications (1), (2), and (3) is that CI dummies are constructed with different percentile cuts. Specification (1) investigates the investment behavior of GPs, whose funds have not achieved a top quartile CI ratio for the two consecutive years preceding the respective transaction. Specifications (2) and (3) do the same for funds, which are not in the top third or above median, respectively. The number of observations slightly drops to 758, accounting for transactions, for which a CI variable could not be calculated due to missing financial information.

A statistically significant result cannot be found for any of the three specifications in the leverage regression on the first stage. However, with the signs of the coefficients being consistently negative across all three specifications, there seems to be a tendency towards low CI funds financing their deals with less leverage than funds with a comparable high CI ratio. With regard to transaction pricing, a positive statistically significant impact of the CI level in specification (1b) can be found (5% level). The result suggests that GPs, which are facing a low CI ratio in comparison to funds of similar age, are paying a 9.7% higher price, than their counterparts. This result is directionally robust, yet not statistically significant, for specifications (2b) and (3b).

Especially the findings for the impact of a fund's CI ratio on the GP's pricing decision, give evidence for the overinvestment problem of the Axelson, et al. (2009) model. If PE firms have not encountered a sufficient number of good firms in early periods of a fund's lifecycle, they pass on bad investments with the hope of being provided with better investment opportunities in the future. Though, due to the incentive structure from their option-like stake in the fund, their willingness to take higher risk increases and so does the likeliness to invest into "too expensive" deals.[143] This is exactly what is shown with the results in Table 10.

---

[143] See Axelson, et al. (2010), p. 14.

Table 10: Capital Invested Regression Results

The table presents the results of the IV2sls regression with CI dummies as explanatory variables. The respective CI dummy variable takes a value of 1 if the fund's CI has not been in the top quartile, the top third or above median for two consecutive years and takes a value of 0 otherwise. All variables not mentioned are the same as used in the previous model. Generally, the numbers in the upper rows represent the regression coefficients. *, ** and *** indicate p-values of 10 %, 5% and 1% significance level, respectively. In the lower rows the detailed t-statistics are reported in parentheses.

VARIABLES	First Stage Log Leverage at Entry			Second Stage Log Multiple at Entry		
	(1a)	(2a)	(3a)	(1b)	(2b)	(3b)
CI (below top quartile)	-0.121			0.097**		
	(-1.38)			(-2.35)		
CI (below top third)		-0.077			0.037	
		(-0.96)			(-0.84)	
CI (below median)			-0.074			0.050
			(-1.20)			(-1.42)
LBO Spreads at Entry	-4.214***	-4.213***	-4.195***			
	(-3.29)	(-3.30)	(-3.30)			
Log Enterprise Value	0.209***	0.209***	0.208***			
	(9.02)	(9.03)	(9.01)			
Log Leverage at Entry				0.659***	0.658***	0.661***
				(-11.35)	(-11.34)	(-11.30)
EBITDA Margin	-0.161*	-0.163*	-0.160*	-0.009	-0.008	-0.009
	(-1.86)	(-1.87)	(-1.85)	(-0.221)	(-0.195)	(-0.219)
Log Multiple Industry	0.015	0.017	0.021	0.08	0.081	0.076
	(0.07)	(0.08)	(0.10)	(-0.77)	(-0.78)	(-0.73)
Log Leverage Industry	0.066	0.065	0.066	-0.012	-0.011	-0.012
	(1.45)	(0.15)	(1.45)	(-0.494)	(-0.466)	(-0.490)
Industries	Yes	Yes	Yes	Yes	Yes	Yes
Regions	Yes	Yes	Yes	Yes	Yes	Yes
Time	Yes	Yes	Yes	Yes	Yes	Yes
Instruments						
LBO Spreads				Yes	Yes	Yes
Enterprise Value				Yes	Yes	Yes
Constant	7.018***	6.951***	6.905***	1.669***	1.740***	1.740***
	(3.02)	(3.00)	(2.99)	(-4.10)	(-4.29)	(-4.30)
Observations	758	758	758	758	758	758
R-squared	0.19	0.19	0.19	0.35	0.35	0.35
F-Statistics	43.90	44.01	43.75			

t-statistics in parentheses
*** p<0.01, ** p<0.05, * p<0.1

Axelson, et al. (2009) further argue that, even though fund managers would probably want to lever up their deals as much as possible, banks would demand for a higher face value of debt given the fund's low CI ratio. As a result, in order to being able to finance marginal investments, ex ante investors need to subsidize ex post financing with an extra portion of equity.[144] This is what can be observed on the first stage in Table 10, however, without being statistically significant.

6.3 Fund Performance Hypothesis

Hypothesis 2 (H2)   *Low fund performance should result in an increased willingness to pay higher prices and*

    a) in higher leverage (independence of GP's leverage decision), or

    b) in lower leverage (limitation of lending capacity).

Table 11 reports the result for IV 2sls regressions using leverage (log EBITDA / Net Debt) and entry multiple (log EV / EBITDA) as dependent and money multiple dummies as independent variables. All other variables are similar to the specification of the basic regression introduced before. The difference between specifications (1), (2), and (3) is similar to the one for CI dummies and accounts for different cutoff points. The number of observations drops to 482, due to the previously discussed exclusion of transactions with performance variables, which are impacted by unrealized deals.

Everything else being equal as in the basic regression, it now can be found a statistically significant impact of fund performance on both leverage and pricing for specifications (1) and (2) (5% level and 10% level, respectively). It cannot be found a significant result for specification (3) in either of the two stages. These results suggest that GPs of funds, which are not facing top returns for the next two consecutive years, finance their deals with less debt, but pay a higher price at the same time. With both absolute coefficients and t-values for the performance dummy decreasing with a broader definition of "top returns", the most meaningful performance cutoff seems to be at the top quartile, i.e. specifications (1a) and (1b). Specifically, the results suggest that top quartile funds use 16.1% more leverage to finance their transactions. At the same time, these funds pay a price that is on average 14.6% lower than the one paid by poor performing funds. The identified cutoff point is consistent with capital market communication practice, which regularly refers to first quartile funds when reporting about top performers.[145]

---

[144] See Axelson, et al. (2009), p. 1568.
[145] See Agrawal (2011), p.1.

The results give evidence for the first part of H2. GPs of poor performing funds are facing the threat of not being able to raise a next generation fund and thus not only lose their current but also potential future compensation. Since the expectation of low fund returns increases the asset substitution problem, they chose their investments less selectively and engage in transactions, for which they are willing to pay a higher price. At the same time, fund performance seems to serve as a short term reputation proxy for outside investors, giving evidence for the lending capacity story of H2 b). The benevolent explanation for this finding is that debt providers know about the overinvestment problem, do not want to take the associated higher risk and thus limit the access to debt for poor performing funds.[146] On the other hand, top quartile funds receive debt financing more easily since GP's do not have an incentive to overinvest. As suggested by the results in Table 11 these GPs then pay even less for their transactions and do not share the rents with the target company's shareholders but use their better access to debt to boost their fund returns even further. This creates a virtuous circle, helping top performing funds to perform even better. Empirical research confirms this observation by showing that a good performance in the early lifetime of a fund is a strong indicator for its future performance. In 50% of the investigated cases, funds in the top quartile remained there until maturity. Only 4% of these funds dropped to bottom quartile performance at the end of their lifecycle.[147] However, the unwillingness of banks to take the higher risk of lending money to GP's, who are incentivized to overinvest, is not the only potential explanation for the findings described above. Another, yet less benevolent and rather opportunistic explanation for lower leverage of poor performing funds goes into the direction of the findings of Ivashina / Kovner (2008). Banks may be willing to provide more favorable credit conditions to funds, if they are expecting future fee business from their investment.[148] Especially PE firms managing top quartile funds can be expected to provide banks with lucrative opportunities to act as an underwriter for IPO's or as a mergers & acquisitions (M&A) advisor. Both the benevolent as well as the opportunistic story are not exclusive and most likely contribute jointly to leverage levels in buyout transactions.

In another regression, it was also investigated whether there is a long term reputation effect on leverage and pricing in addition to the identified effect of fund performance as a short-term reputation proxy. Adding the natural logarithms of fund generation, fund manager age and AUM (5y) to the regression depicted in Table 11 no significant results can be found for either leverage or pricing. These findings suggest that a short-term reputation measure in the form of fund performance serves as a more important signal to outside investors than a measure calculated on the basis of long-term indicators. The results of this regression are shown in Table 14 in Appendix 4.

---

[146] See Axelson, et al. (2009), p. 1568.
[147] See Preqin Ltd. (2011), p. 2.
[148] See Ivashina / Kovner (2008), p. 3.

A potential weakness of the leverage explanation above is the fact that it assumes GP's to be able to somehow make credible statements about their future fund performance to outside investors.[149] However, it can be assumed that a GP only states a high fund performance if this is actually the case. If a GP of a bad performing fund imitated a good performing fund only to get a higher amount of debt, this behavior would backfire as soon as it turns out that he was not saying the truth. As a result, the trustful relationship with debt providers would be destroyed, potentially translating into a less lenient debt provision and the demand for much stricter covenants for all future investments.[150] GPs, who are not only worried about their current but also their future compensation, would most certainly avoid running into that kind of predictable disadvantage.[151]

Another notable caveat of the explanation stems from the closely linked relationship between leverage and performance. It is the very basic idea of an LBO to boost equity returns through the employment of large amounts of debt. In general, the higher the debt ratio in an LBO transaction, the higher is the return on equity from that investment.[152] While the argument provided in this study claims that the higher leverage in a specific transaction is a result of the performance of prior investments, a reverse relationship cannot be fully ruled out. A potential approach to circumvent this problem might be an alternative specification of the IV 2sls regression with leverage as dependent variable on the second stage. By instrumenting a fund performance variable with other value drivers, such as operational improvement measures, the impact of overall fund performance on deal level leverage could be quantified more precisely.[153] Unfortunately, this analysis goes beyond the scope of this study, but would be an interesting topic for future research.

---

[149] This is the case, because performance dummies included into the regression are based on "expected", future and not on actual, realized fund returns. Credible statements about fund performance must be made specifically to ex post investors, as ex ante capital is generally already committed at the beginning of the fund lifecycle.

[150] See Ivashina / Kovner (2008), p. 6.

[151] A formal explanation of a GP's incentive structure using advanced topics of game theory would go beyond the scope of this study. For further readings please refer to Kreps / Wilson (1982) and Grossman / Perry (1986) for the sequential equilibrium concept.

[152] See Modigliani / Miller (1958), p. 271.

[153] See Achleitner / Figge (2011), p. 3; The authors refer to operating performance, leverage, and pricing as major value creation drivers in leveraged buyouts.

Table 11: Performance Regression Results

The table presents the results of the IV2sls regression with performance dummies as explanatory variables. The respective performance dummy variable takes a value of 1 if the fund's performance has not been in the top quartile, the top third or above median for two consecutive years and takes a value of 0 otherwise. Performance is measured with money multiples. All variables not mentioned are the same as used in the previous model. Generally, the numbers in the upper rows represent the regression coefficients. *, ** and *** indicate p-values of 10 %, 5% and 1% significance level, respectively. In the lower rows the detailed t-statistics are reported in parentheses.

VARIABLES	First Stage Log Leverage at Entry			Second Stage Log Multiple at Entry		
	(1a)	(2a)	(3a)	(1b)	(2b)	(3b)
Perf. (below top quartile)	-0.161**			0.146**		
	(-1.98)			(-2.50)		
Perf. (below top third)		-0.158*			0.110*	
		(-1.75)			(-1.77)	
Perf. (below median)			0.074			0.044
			(-0.84)			(-0.77)
LBO Spreads at Entry	-5.781***	-5.807***	-5.749***			
	(-4.99)	(-5.03)	(-4.95)			
Log Enterprise Value	0.161***	0.160***	0.161***			
	(5.69)	(5.65)	(5.64)			
Log Leverage at Entry				0.743***	0.746***	0.741***
				(-7.40)	(-7.28)	(-7.20)
EBITDA Margin	-0.127	-0.130	-0.133	-0.006	-0.003	-0.002
	(-1.16)	(-1.19)	(-1.21)	(-0.10)	(-0.06)	(-0.04)
Log Multiple Industry	0.232	0.229	0.209	-0.018	-0.013	0.001
	(0.91)	(0.90)	(0.83)	(-0.13)	(-0.10)	(-0.01)
Log Leverage Industry	0.106*	0.104*	0.111*	0.005	0.005	0.000
	(1.81)	(1.78)	(1.92)	(-0.15)	(-0.13)	(-0.01)
Industries	Yes	Yes	Yes	Yes	Yes	Yes
Regions	Yes	Yes	Yes	Yes	Yes	Yes
Time	Yes	Yes	Yes	Yes	Yes	Yes
Instruments						
LBO Spreads				Yes	Yes	Yes
Enterprise Value				Yes	Yes	Yes
Constant	10.018***	10.255***	10.044***	1.301***	1.311***	1.393***
	(4.33)	(4.49)	(4.35)	(-3.02)	(-3.03)	(-3.23)
Observations	482	482	482	482	482	482
R-squared	0.15	0.15	0.14	0.27	0.26	0.26
F-Statistics	32.28	32.24	31.85			

t-statistics in parentheses
*** p<0.01, ** p<0.05, * p<0.1

An important question arising from the findings above is how CI impacts performance effects and vice versa. If there is an interaction effect between the CI and the performance variable, different results must be obtained for poor performing funds with a low in contrast to funds with a high CI ratio. If there is no interaction, the effect is additive and low performing funds simply use less leverage and pay more regardless of their CI ratio. To test whether or not an interaction effect is existent, interaction terms have been created for both below top quartile and below median funds with regard to performance and CI, respectively. The regression statistics for all of these interactions are depicted in

Table 12. According to the results above, the largest effect should be observable for funds, which are facing both below quartile CI and performance. Indeed, the interaction term for specification (1b) is statistically significant, though only on the 10% level. For a robust interaction effect, there should be at least a tendency towards the results from (1b) in specifications (2b) to (4b). However, while specification (1b) indicates a negative effect on pricing for a poorly performing fund with low CI ratio, this effect turns around for specifications (2b), (3b) and (4b).[154] The results indicate that a model without the interaction might be better fitted. Specifications (5a) and (5b) depict the results of the additive model. CI and performance dummies are statistically significant for both specifications and imply a negative relation to leverage (both 5% level) and a positive relation to entry pricing (10% level for performance and 5% level for CI dummy), just as in the individual analyses above. Also, the quantitative impact changes only slightly. Controlling for the performance level, funds with low CI use 20.7% less leverage (not significant in the individual analysis) and pay a 10.2% higher price (9.7%). Likewise, when controlling for the level of CI, funds with low performance use 14.6% less leverage (16.1%) and pay a price that is 13.1% higher (14.6%).

The results suggest that both variables are independently influencing leverage and pricing. A low CI ratio implies that the GP did not encounter enough investment opportunities and, independently from the fund's performance, has the incentive to overinvest. On the other hand, if the GP is facing poor performance, the willingness to take higher risk should not significantly differ in case of different CI ratios.

---

[154] The effect on the entry multiple of a poorly performing fund is calculated by adding up the coefficients of all three explanatory variables. For (1b) this would be: $-0.179 - 0.185 + 0.332 = -0.032$. The same calculation for specifications (2b) to (4b) yields 0.114, 0.188 and 0.059, respectively.

Table 12: Interaction Regression Results

The table presents the results of the IV2sls regression with CI dummies, performance dummies and their interaction as explanatory variables. The variables are defined the same as before. All variables not mentioned are the same as used in the previous models. Generally, the numbers in the upper rows represent the regression coefficients. *, ** and *** indicate p-values of 10 %, 5% and 1% significance level, respectively. In the lower rows the detailed t-statistics are reported in parentheses.

	First Stage					Second Stage				
	Log Leverage at Entry					Log Multiple at Entry				
VARIABLES	(1a)	(2a)	(3a)	(4a)	(5a)	(1b)	(2b)	(3b)	(4b)	(5b)
Perf. (below top quartile)	0.014	-0.010			-0.146*	-0.179	0.101			0.131**
	(0.06)	(-0.08)			(-1.73)	(-1.13)	(-1.26)			(-2.15)
Perf. (below median)			-0.117	-0.093				0.128	0.087	
			(-0.62)	(-0.63)				(-1.18)	(-0.93)	
CI (below top quartile)	-0.058		-0.258*		-0.207*	-0.185		0.171*		0.102*
	(-0.26)		(-1.92)		(-1.87)	(-1.18)		(-1.84)		(-1.77)
CI (below median)		0.045		-0.130			-0.028		0.048	
		(0.34)		(-1.11)			(-0.30)		(-0.64)	
Interaction Term	-0.171	-0.177	0.080	0.062		0.332*	0.041	-0.111	-0.076	
	(-0.66)	(-1.05)	(0.39)	(0.39)		(-1.87)	(-0.34)	(-0.97)	(-0.76)	
LBO Spreads at Entry	-6.091***	-6.158***	-6.028***	-6.026***	-6.067***					
	(-5.57)	(-5.65)	(-5.48)	(-5.50)	(-5.55)					
Log Enterprise Value	0.153***	0.152***	0.154***	0.152***	0.154***					
	(5.59)	(5.56)	(5.57)	(5.50)	(5.63)					
Log Leverage at Entry						0.765***	0.766***	0.761***	0.767***	0.763***
						(-7.18)	(-7.04)	(-6.99)	(-6.96)	(-7.19)
EBITDA Margin	-0.123	-0.120	-0.126	-0.127	-0.123	0.004	0.001	0.004	0.005	0.002
	(-1.11)	(-1.08)	(-1.14)	(-1.13)	(-1.11)	(-0.07)	(-0.02)	(-0.07)	(-0.10)	(-0.05)
Log Multiple Industry	0.213	0.213	0.190	0.191	0.209	-0.046	-0.034	-0.021	-0.019	-0.038
	(0.83)	(0.82)	(0.75)	(0.75)	(0.82)	(-0.32)	(-0.24)	(-0.15)	(-0.14)	(-0.271)
Log Leverage Industry	0.097	0.095	0.103*	0.103*	0.098*	0.001	0.002	-0.005	-0.004	0.000
	(1.63)	(1.58)	(1.75)	(1.74)	(1.65)	(-0.03)	(-0.06)	(-0.12)	(-0.10)	(-0.01)
Industries	Yes	Yes	Yes	Yes	Yes	Yes	Yes	Yes	Yes	Yes
Regions	Yes	Yes	Yes	Yes	Yes	Yes	Yes	Yes	Yes	Yes
Time	Yes	Yes	Yes	Yes	Yes	Yes	Yes	Yes	Yes	Yes
Instruments										
LBO Spreads						Yes	Yes	Yes	Yes	Yes
Enterprise Value						Yes	Yes	Yes	Yes	Yes
Constant	10.769***	10.778***	10.763***	10.608***	10.867***	1.522***	1.378***	1.274***	1.401***	1.254***
	(4.82)	(4.87)	(4.80)	(4.79)	(4.89)	(-3.26)	(-3.08)	(-2.76)	(-3.09)	(-2.77)
Observations	457	557	457	457	457	457	457	457	457	457
R-squared	0.17	0.16	0.16	0.16	0.17	0.22	0.21	0.21	0.20	0.22
F-Statistics	33.52	33.98	32.24	32.50	33.46					

t-statistics in parentheses
*** p<0.01, ** p<0.05, * p<0.1

6.4 Reputation Effects Hypothesis

Hypothesis 3 (H3) *The effects of H1 and H2 should be stronger for GPs with low reputation.*

If a PE firm's reputation is amplifying the effects described in the previous sections, it should be identifiable through a regression analysis that includes interaction terms of a reputation measure and the respective CI and performance dummy. Results for this analysis are presented in Table 13. The regressions depicted in the table comprise the natural logarithms of fund generation, PE firm age at entry and AUM as reputation measures as well as their interaction with CI and performance dummies. In each of the three different specifications, below top quartile dummies were used for both performance and CI variables.

For fund generation and PE firm age, significant results can neither be found on the first, nor on the second stage. For these two specifications LBO spreads lose their significance and the sign even turns positive for the fund generation regression in (1a). To test whether this result is robust, the same regression analysis was conducted with first time fund and low fund age dummies as reputation variables. These specifications yield similar, non-significant, results and are depicted in Table 15 in Appendix 4. Even though, significant results on the first stage cannot be found for the impact of AUM in (3a), at least LBO spreads are again negative and significant on the 5% level. On the second stage, both the CI interaction term (10% level) and the performance dummy (10% level) are significantly impacting the dependent variable. These results suggest the existence of an amplifying effect of a PE firm's long-term reputation on investment pressure variables. However, to be sure that this finding is sustainable, a couple of robustness checks need to be conducted. A joint test of the two interaction coefficients rejects the null hypothesis of both being jointly zero at the 5% level and yields an F-statistic of 6.84. These results are more significant than for the previously rejected interaction effect without reputation impact. However, R-squared drops to 9.5% from above 20% in specifications (1b) and (2b). To further test whether the results obtained in specification (3b) are robust, the same regression was conducted for fund size as a reputation measure. Fund size is highly correlated to AUM and thus should yield similar results.[155] Unfortunately, this is not the case. Specifically, none of the interaction variables are any significant, the joint test of the two interaction coefficients yields a p-value of 0.49 (F-statistics: 1.41), and the R-squared on the second stage drops even further to below 4%.

Consequently, an interaction effect cannot be identified and, at least for the results obtained from the investigated dataset, the reputation hypothesis as such must be rejected. Low long term reputation does not seem to intensify the effects of investment pressure. The results of an additive analysis are reported in Table 16 in Appendix 4. Similar to the previously discussed results of the long-term reputation regression for the performance dummy (Table 14), an additive effect can neither be identified. However, signs and significance for both CI and performance dummies remain fairly robust, giving further evidence for the identified dynamics in a fund manager's investment behavior.

---

[155] The correlation for absolute values of fund size and AUM is 0.66. The correlation coefficient for the natural logarithms of both variables, which are used in the regression analysis, is 0.84.

Table 13: Reputation Regression Results

The table presents the results of the IV2sls regression with CI dummies, performance dummies and their interaction with reputation measures as explanatory variables. Log Fund Generation and log Age of PE firm are the natural logarithm of the respective variable. Log AUM 5y is the natural logarithm of the accumulated committed capital raised in the five years prior to the transaction. All variables not mentioned are the same as used in the previous models. Generally, the numbers in the upper rows represent the regression coefficients. *, ** and *** indicate p-values of 10 %, 5% and 1% significance level, respectively. In the lower rows the detailed t-statistics are reported in parentheses.

	First Stage Log Leverage at Entry			Second Stage Log Multiple at Entry		
VARIABLES	(1a)	(2a)	(3a)	(1b)	(2b)	(3b)
Perf. (below top quartile)	-0.019	0.304	-0.172	0.013	-0.069	0.518*
	(-0.12)	(0.78)	(-0.40)	(-0.14)	(-0.32)	(-1.72)
CI (below top quartile)	-0.144	-0.071	-0.232	0.096	0.214	-0.334
	(-0.54)	(-0.14)	(-0.53)	(-0.75)	(-0.66)	(-1.39)
Log Fund Generation	0.244			-0.054		
	(1.01)			(-0.48)		
Log Age of PE firm		0.271			-0.019	
		(1.24)			(-0.15)	
Log AUM 5y			-0.058			-0.021
			(-0.89)			(-0.30)
Perf. Interaction Term	-0.141	-0.194	0.002	0.129	0.084	-0.055
	(-0.82)	(-1.16)	(0.03)	(-1.28)	(-0.87)	(-1.09)
CI Interaction Term	-0.065	-0.058	0.011	0.005	-0.045	0.062*
	(-0.31)	(-0.31)	(0.20)	(-0.05)	(-0.38)	(-1.91)
LBO Spreads at Entry	1.298	-1.389	-1.830**			
	(0.70)	(-1.02)	(-2.13)			
Log Enterprise Value	0.160***	0.164***	0.169***			
	(5.57)	(5.60)	(4.88)			
Log Leverage at Entry				0.733***	0.761***	0.817***
				(-7.08)	(-7.27)	(-6.08)
EBITDA Margin	-0.137	-0.134	-0.133	0.013	0.008	0.02
	(-1.20)	(-1.19)	(-1.17)	(-0.24)	(-0.14)	(-0.30)
Log Multiple Industry	0.214	0.220	0.315	-0.049	-0.042	-0.149
	(0.83)	(0.87)	(1.24)	(-0.36)	(-0.30)	(-1.02)
Log Leverage Industry	0.093	0.093	0.091	0.004	0.005	-0.013
	(1.54)	(1.51)	(1.41)	(-0.09)	(-0.13)	(-0.26)
Industries	Yes	Yes	Yes	Yes	Yes	Yes
Regions	Yes	Yes	Yes	Yes	Yes	Yes
Time	Yes	Yes	Yes	Yes	Yes	Yes
Instruments						
LBO Spreads				Yes	Yes	Yes
Enterprise Value				Yes	Yes	Yes
Constant	-2.615	2.166	3.187**	1.375***	1.192**	1.680***
	(-0.80)	(0.80)	(2.48)	(-3.15)	(-2.15)	(-3.41)
Observations	454	456	431	454	456	431
R-squared	0.17	0.17	0.17	0.27	0.22	0.10
F-Statistics	15.70	17.75	12.20			

t-statistics in parentheses
*** p<0.01, ** p<0.05, * p<0.1

7 Conclusion

Private equity firms, and especially leveraged buyouts, are becoming increasingly important for both companies and investors. However, mostly due to the restricted access to information on relevant variables, there is only a limited amount of quantitative research on the structure of buyout investments. Especially the impact of investment pressure on leverage and pricing in LBOs is not covered sufficiently by existing empirical literature. This study provides the first comprehensive empirical analysis on how buyout fund dynamics influence investment structuring decisions of fund managers. Thereby, it was relied on a representative dataset of 1,190 buyout transactions completed between 1985 and 2009. Also, already identified determinants of leverage and pricing have been considered and appropriately controlled for in the regression analyses.

The results of this study clearly suggest that fund managers, who are "behind the curve" and thus face an increased investment pressure, do structure their investments differently than their counterparts. However, especially the decision on the amount of debt used to finance the transaction is strongly influenced by debt capital providers, who actively determine the accessibility of debt financing.

In line with the predictions of the Axelson, et al. (2009) model, the study finds that a consecutively low CI ratio leads to lower leverage and higher entry multiples. Having faced a period with only a limited number of good investment opportunities, the fund managers' incentive to overinvest increases and so does their willingness to do marginal deals at higher prices. Debt capital providers are aware of this behavior and therefore lend money at stricter conditions. In turn, fund managers are forced to finance their deals with a larger equity fraction. In addition to the findings regarding a fund's CI ratio, it is also found that the same dynamics apply for poor performance. Funds, that are expected to perform not in the top quartile for the two consecutive years after the respective transaction, use less leverage and accept higher entry multiples. The findings indicate that in an effort to turn around their fund's performance, fund managers tend to overinvest and pay higher prices for prospective portfolio companies. At the same time, debt providers refrain to lend an excessive amount of capital to fund these transactions. As opposed to this, good performing funds receive better access to leverage and pay lower entry multiples, which creates a virtuous circle, making good performing funds even better. The effects for CI and performance are additive and do not influence each other. Even though, various authors suggest that both effects should be stronger for younger PE firms,[156] this cannot be confirmed on the basis of the identified results and must be rejected.

The findings of this study open up a number of further research possibilities. Firstly, as discussed, the endogeneity problem between fund performance and leverage could be addressed with an alternative specification. Secondly, as this study could not exclusively answer the question about the main motivation behind a debt provider's decision to limit

---

[156] See Axelson, et al. (2009), p. 1572; Chung, et al. (2010), p. 3; Ljungqvist, et al. (2008), pp. 23f.

capital access for poor performing funds, it might be worthwhile to have a closer look at this subject. Thirdly, as the dataset did not allow for the development of risk measures for each individual transaction, the inclusion of such risk measures would help to further support the findings regarding the overinvestment behavior of fund managers. In general, this study can serve as a fruitful basis for these topics.

Appendix

Appendix 1: Industry reference table

Industry Classification Benchmark (ICB)	Strömberg (2008), p. 32.
Oil & Gas	Energy
Basic Materials	Metals and Mining, Steel
	Chemicals, Industrial, and Agricultural Products, Paper and Forest Products
Industrials	Industrial Machinery
	Advanced Industrial Equipment
	Industrial and Commercial Services
	Industrial and Construction Materials
	Transportation
	Construction and Engineering
	Education, Human Resource and Employment Services
Consumer Goods	Food, Beverages, and Tobacco
	Automotive
	Household Durables
	Household Non-Durables
Health Care	Healthcare Products and Equipment
	Healthcare Services and Providers
	Biotech, Pharmaceuticals, Life Sciences
Consumer Services	Retail
	Hotels, Resorts and Cruise Lines, Leisure Facilities, Restaurants
	Media, Publishing, Advertising
	Trading Companies and Distributors
	Movies and Entertainment
Telecommunications	IT and Data Service
	Computer and Telecommunications Equipment
	Telecom
Utilities	Infrastructure and Utilities
Financials	Financials
	Real Estate
Technology	Software and Internet
Not categorized	Multi-Sector Holdings and Conglomerates
	Other Services

Appendix 2: Time series data[157]

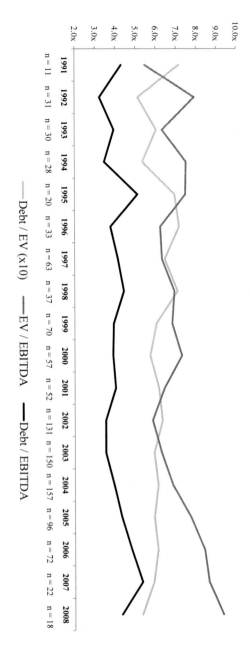

[157] Own source. Data before 1991 as well as data from 2009 intentionally left out due to the low number of observations.

Appendix 3: Fund statistics[158]

Money multiple statistics by fund age

	3	4	5	6	7	8	9	10	11	12	13	14	15
n	236	335	394	400	379	352	323	290	263	241	241	240	235
min	0.0	0.0	0.0	0.0	0.0	0.0	0.0	0.0	0.7	0.6	0.6	0.6	0.6
p25	0.0	0.7	1.1	1.4	1.6	1.8	1.9	2.0	2.1	2.1	2.1	2.1	2.1
med	1.5	1.9	2.1	2.3	2.5	2.6	2.7	2.8	2.9	2.9	2.9	2.8	2.9
mean	2.2	2.4	2.7	3.1	3.5	3.5	3.6	3.6	3.7	3.8	3.6	3.7	3.7
p75	2.5	3.2	3.3	3.6	3.8	3.8	3.9	4.0	4.0	4.0	4.0	4.1	4.1
max	34.1	18.4	27.6	46.1	165.3	87.8	87.8	87.8	87.8	87.8	52.7	52.7	52.7

CI statistics by fund age

	1	2	3	4	5	6	7	8	9	10
n	644	625	576	528	492	459	412	374	338	299
min	0.00	0.00	0.00	0.01	0.01	0.03	0.06	0.06	0.06	0.16
p25	0.02	0.16	0.33	0.48	0.64	0.77	0.83	0.86	0.87	0.86
med	0.08	0.28	0.49	0.66	0.83	0.90	0.94	0.97	0.97	0.98
mean	0.12	0.32	0.51	0.66	0.77	0.84	0.88	0.89	0.90	0.90
p75	0.17	0.43	0.69	0.85	0.93	0.96	0.99	1.00	1.00	1.00
max	1.00	1.00	1.00	1.00	1.00	1.00	1.00	1.00	1.00	1.00

---

[158] Own source.

Appendix 4: Regression results

Table 14: Long Term Reputation Regression Results

The table presents the results of the IV2sls regression with performance dummies and reputation measures as explanatory variables. The performance dummy relies on money multiples and takes a value of 1 if the respective fund did not perform in the top quartile performance for two years in a row after the entry year and 0 otherwise. Log Fund Generation and log Age of PE firm are the natural logarithm of the respective variable. Log AUM 5y is the natural logarithm of the accumulated committed capital raised in the five years prior the transaction. All variables not mentioned are the same as used in the previous models. Generally, the numbers in the upper rows represent the regression coefficients. *, ** and *** indicate p-values of 10 %, 5% and 1% significance level, respectively. In the lower rows the detailed t-statistics are reported in parentheses.

VARIABLES	First Stage Log Leverage at Entry			Second Stage Log Multiple at Entry		
	(1a)	(2a)	(3a)	(1b)	(2b)	(3b)
Perf. (below top quartile)	-0.159*	-0.173**	-0.205**	0.154***	0.149**	0.171***
	(-1.95)	(-2.14)	(-2.18)	(-2.68)	(-2.51)	(-2.67)
Log Fund Generation	0.093			0.039		
	(1.25)			(-0.94)		
Log Age of PE firm		0.055			0.010	
		(0.85)			(-0.33)	
Log AUM 5y			-0.046			-0.012
			(-1.06)			(-0.44)
LBO Spreads at Entry	-0.035	-0.104	0.206*			
	(-0.22)	(-0.66)	(1.65)			
Log Enterprise Value	0.161***	0.163***	0.174***			
	(5.73)	(5.77)	(5.12)			
Log Leverage at Entry				0.745***	0.760***	0.754***
				(-7.55)	(-7.59)	(-6.54)
EBITDA Margin	-0.134	-0.124	-0.129	0.001	-0.004	0.006
	(-1.21)	(-1.14)	(-1.14)	(-0.01)	(-0.07)	(-0.11)
Log Multiple Industry	0.232	0.233	0.301	-0.029	-0.031	-0.100
	(0.93)	(0.92)	(1.18)	(-0.21)	(-0.23)	(-0.73)
Log Leverage Industry	0.104*	0.108*	0.075	0.002	0.006	-0.002
	(1.78)	(1.84)	(1.18)	(-0.07)	(-0.16)	(-0.04)
Industries	Yes	Yes	Yes	Yes	Yes	Yes
Regions	Yes	Yes	Yes	Yes	Yes	Yes
Time	Yes	Yes	Yes	Yes	Yes	Yes
Instruments						
LBO Spreads				Yes	Yes	Yes
Enterprise Value				Yes	Yes	Yes
Constant	-0.040	0.135	-0.810	1.240***	1.195***	1.508***
	(-0.06)	(0.19)	(-1.38)	(-3.34)	(-3.18)	(-3.75)
Observations	479	481	441	479	481	441
R-squared	0.15	0.15	0.16	0.27	0.24	0.17
F-Statistics	21.97	19.50	17.35			

t-statistics in parentheses
*** p<0.01, ** p<0.05, * p<0.1

Table 15: Reputation Dummy Regression Results

The table presents the results of the IV2sls with CI dummies, performance dummies and their interaction with reputation measures as explanatory variables. The performance dummy relies on money multiples and takes a value of 1 if the respective fund did not perform in the top quartile performance for two years in a row after the entry year and 0 otherwise. The CI dummy variable takes a value of 1 if the fund's CI has not been in the top quartile for the two consecutive years prior the entry year and takes a value of 0 otherwise. The Young Firm Dummy takes a value of 1 if the PE firm is younger than 6 years and 0 otherwise. The First Time Fund Dummy takes a value of 1 if it is the first generation fund and 0 otherwise. All variables not mentioned are the same as used in the previous models. Generally, the numbers in the upper rows represent the regression coefficients. *, ** and *** indicate p-values of 10 %, 5% and 1% significance level, respectively. In the lower rows the detailed t-statistics are reported in parentheses.

VARIABLES	First Stage Log Leverage at Entry		Second Stage Log Multiple at Entry	
	(1a)	(2a)	(1b)	(2b)
Perf. (below top quartile)	-0.167*	-0.168	0.124*	0.146*
	(-1.76)	(-1.53)	(-1.78)	(-1.94)
CI (below top quartile)	-0.199*	-0.242**	0.097*	0.121**
	(-1.74)	(-2.09)	(-1.66)	(-2.06)
Young Firm Dummy	0.002		-0.246	
	(0.01)		(-1.426)	
First Time Fund Dummy		-0.310		0.077
		(-0.78)		(-0.44)
Perf. Interaction Term	0.114	0.077	0.105	0.001
	(0.48)	(0.36)	(-0.77)	(-0.01)
CI Interaction Term	-0.116	0.246	0.192	-0.146
	(-0.40)	(0.64)	(-1.13)	(-0.868)
LBO Spreads at Entry	-1.678	1.307		
	(-1.19)	(0.65)		
Log Enterprise Value	0.156***	0.155***		
	(5.43)	(5.46)		
Log Leverage at Entry			0.789***	0.760***
			(-7.07)	(-6.94)
EBITDA Margin	-0.124	-0.128	0.004	0.008
	(-1.12)	(-1.14)	(-0.08)	(-0.15)
Log Multiple Industry	0.223	0.215	-0.046	-0.044
	(0.88)	(0.84)	(-0.318)	(-0.314)
Log Leverage Industry	0.095	0.097	-0.003	-0.001
	(1.56)	(1.61)	(-0.078)	(-0.015)
Industries	Yes	Yes	Yes	Yes
Regions	Yes	Yes	Yes	Yes
Time	Yes	Yes	Yes	Yes
Instruments				
LBO Spreads	Yes	Yes	Yes	Yes
Enterprise Value	Yes	Yes	Yes	Yes
Constant	3.288	-2.425	1.114***	1.285***
	(1.24)	(-0.67)	(-2.70)	(-3.21)
Observations	457	455	457	455
R-squared	0.17	0.17	0.18	0.23
F-Statistics	17.56	15.11		

t-statistics in parentheses
*** p<0.01, ** p<0.05, * p<0.1

Table 16: Additive Long Term Reputation Regression Results

The table presents the results of the IV2sls with CI dummies, performance dummies and different reputation measures as explanatory variables. All variables are the same as used in the previous models. Generally, the numbers in the upper rows represent the regression coefficients. *, ** and *** indicate p-values of 10 %, 5% and 1% significance level, respectively. In the lower rows the detailed t-statistics are reported in parentheses.

VARIABLES	First Stage Regression Leverage at Entry					Second Stage Regression Multiple at Entry				
	(1a)	(2a)	(3a)	(4a)	(5a)	(1b)	(2b)	(3b)	(4b)	(5b)
Perf. (below top quartile)	-0.150*	-0.157*	-0.161*	-0.147*	-0.146*	0.137**	0.136**	0.148**	0.143**	0.137**
	(-1.77)	(-1.89)	(-1.75)	(-1.69)	(-1.75)	(-2.30)	(-2.20)	(-2.32)	(-2.40)	(-2.26)
CI (below top quartile)	-0.208*	-0.220*	-0.156	-0.207*	-0.208*	0.104*	0.100*	0.093	0.103*	0.102*
	(-1.88)	(-1.94)	(-1.38)	(-1.86)	(-1.88)	(-1.81)	(-1.70)	(-1.62)	(-1.78)	(-1.74)
Log Fund Generation	0.066					0.055				
	(0.93)					(-1.31)				
Log Age of PE firm		0.062					0.005			
		(0.89)					(-0.16)			
Log AUM 5y			-0.047					-0.011		
			(-1.09)					(-0.40)		
First Time Fund Dummy				-0.019					-0.059	
				(-0.20)					(-1.02)	
Young Fund Dummy					-0.028					0.006
					(-0.26)					(-0.10)
LBO Spreads at Entry	-0.041	-0.143	0.185	-0.003	-0.085					
	(-0.26)	(-0.91)	(1.52)	(-0.02)	(-0.61)					
Log Enterprise Value	0.155***	0.156***	0.169***	0.154***	0.154***					
	(5.63)	(5.71)	(5.18)	(5.64)	(5.66)					
Log Leverage at Entry						0.769***	0.784***	0.784***	0.762***	0.781***
						(-7.36)	(-7.37)	(-6.54)	(-7.37)	(-7.39)
EBITDA Margin	-0.128	-0.119	-0.133	-0.126	-0.122	0.009	0.004	0.015	0.008	0.005
	(-1.15)	(-1.09)	(-1.17)	(-1.14)	(-1.10)	(-0.17)	(-0.07)	(-0.25)	(-0.15)	(-0.08)
Log Multiple Industry	0.210	0.215	0.308	0.217	0.217	-0.052	-0.052	-0.128	-0.042	-0.048
	(0.84)	(0.85)	(1.22)	(0.87)	(0.86)	(-0.36)	(-0.36)	(-0.90)	(-0.30)	(-0.34)
Log Leverage Industry	0.095	0.100*	0.091	0.098*	0.098	-0.004	0.001	-0.011	-0.001	0.000
	(1.63)	(1.68)	(1.43)	(1.66)	(1.65)	(-0.10)	(-0.02)	(-0.23)	(-0.02)	(-0.00)
Industries	Yes	Yes	Yes	Yes	Yes	Yes	Yes	Yes	Yes	Yes
Regions	Yes	Yes	Yes	Yes	Yes	Yes	Yes	Yes	Yes	Yes
Time	Yes	Yes	Yes	Yes	Yes	Yes	Yes	Yes	Yes	Yes
Instruments										
LBO Spreads						Yes	Yes	Yes	Yes	Yes
Enterprise Value						Yes	Yes	Yes	Yes	Yes
Constant	0.130	0.397	-0.651	0.043	0.344	1.227***	1.184***	1.499***	1.276***	1.177***
	(0.19)	(0.57)	(1.11)	(0.06)	(0.48)	(-3.22)	(-3.08)	(-3.67)	(-3.30)	(-2.98)
Observations	454	456	431	455	457	454	456	431	455	457
R-squared	0.17	0.17	0.17	0.17	0.16	0.22	0.19	0.15	0.23	0.19
F-Statistics	22.23	18.90	16.68	21.51	19.44					

t-statistics in parentheses
*** p<0.01, ** p<0.05, * p<0.1

References

Acharya, V. V. / Hahn, M. / Kehoe, K. (2010): Corporate Governance and value Creation: Evidence from Private Equity, Working Paper, 1-65

Achleitner, A.-K. / Braun, R. / Engel, N. (2011): Value Creation and Pricing in Buyouts: Empirical Evidence from Europe and North America, Center for Entrepreneurial and Financial Studies Working Paper, 1-41

Achleitner, A.-K. / Braun, R. / Engel, N. / Figge, C. / Tappeiner, F. (2010a): Value Creation Drivers in Private Equity Buyouts: Empirical Evidence from Europe, Journal of Private Equity, 13 (2), 1-12

Achleitner, A.-K. / Braun, R. / Hinterramskogler, B. / Tappeiner, F. (2010b): Structure and Determinants of Financial Covenants in Leveraged Buyouts, Center for Entrepreneurial and Financial Studies Working Paper No. 2009-15 1-49

Achleitner, A.-K. / Figge, C. (2011): Private Equity Lemons? Evidence on Value Creation in Secondary Buyouts, Working Paper, 1-40

Axelson, U. / Jenkinson, T. / Stromberg, P. J. / Weisbach, M. S. (2010): Borrow Cheap, Buy High? The Determinants of Leverage and Pricing in Buyouts, Working Paper, 1-66

Axelson, U. / Strömberg, P. / Weisbach, M. S. (2009): Why Are Buyouts Levered? The Financial Structure of Private Equity Funds, Journal of Finance, 64 (4), 1549-1582

Baum, C. F. (2006): An Introduction to Modern Econometrics using Stata, 2006

Blaydon, C. / Wainwright, F. (2003): Note on Limited Partnership Agreements, Working Paper, 1-7

Board of Governors of the Federal Reserve System (2011): Economic Research & Data, http://www.federalreserve.gov/econresdata/ (2011-02-14)

Cho, I.-K. / Kreps, D. M. (1987): Signaling Games and Stable Equilibria, Quarterly Journal of Economics, 102 (2), 179-221

Chung, J.-W. / Sensoy, B. A. / Stern, L. H. / Weisbach, M. S. (2010): Pay for Performance from Future Fund Flows: The Case of Private Equity, NBER Working Papers, 1-38

Demiroglu, C. / James, C. M. (2010): The role of private equity group reputation in LBO financing, Journal of Financial Economics, 96 (2), 306-330

Dow Jones Indexes (2011): Industry Classification Benchmark, http://www.icbenchmark.com (2011-02-15)

EVCA (2010): EVCA Buyout Report, EVCA Research Papers, 1-68

Gompers, P. / Lerner, J. (1996): The Use of Covenants: An Empirical Analysis of Venture Partnership Agreements, Journal of Law & Economics, 39 (2), 463-498

Gompers, P. / Lerner, J. (1999): An analysis of compensation in the U.S. venture capital partnership, Journal of Financial Economics, 51 (1), 3-44

Gompers, P. A. (1995): Optimal Investment, Monitoring, and the Staging of Venture Capital, Journal of Finance, 50 (5), 1461-1489

Grossman, S. J. / Perry, M. (1986): Perfect Sequential Equilibrium, Journal of Economic Theory, 39 (1), 97-119

Ivashina, V. / Kovner, A. (2008): The Private Equity Advantage: Leveraged Buyout Firms and Relationship Banking, Working Paper, 1-61

Jensen, M. C. (1989): Eclipse of the Public Corporation, Harvard Business Review, 61-74

Jensen, M. C. / Meckling, W. H. (1976): Theory of the firm: Managerial Behavior, Agency Costs and Ownership Structure, Journal of Financial Economics, 3 (4), 305-360

Kaplan, S. (1989): Management Buyouts: Evidence on Taxes as a Source of Value, Journal of Finance, 44 (3), 611-632

Kaplan, S. N. / Schoar, A. (2005): Private Equity Performance: Returns, Persistence, and Capital Flows, Journal of Finance, 60 (4), 1791-1823

Kaplan, S. N. / Stein, J. C. (1993): The evolution of buyout pricing and financial structure in the 1980s, Quarterly Journal of Economics, 108 (2), 313-257

Kaplan, S. N. / Strömberg, P. (2009): Leveraged Buyouts and Private Equity, Journal of Economic Perspectives, 23 (1), 121-146

Kreps, D. M. / Wilson, R. (1982): Sequential Equilibria, Econometrica, 50 (4), 863-894

Leland, H. E. (1994): Corporate Debt Value, Bond Covenants, and Optimal Capital Structure. (cover story), Journal of Finance, 49 (4), 1213-1252

Ljungqvist, A. / Richardson, M. P. / Wolfenzon, D. (2008): The Investment Behavior of Buyout Funds: Theory and Evidence, ECGI working Paper Series in Finance, 1-41

Lopez de Silanes, F. / Phalippou, L. / Gottschalg, O. (2009): Giants at the Gate: On the Cross-Section of Private Equity Investment Returns, Working Paper, 1-67

Maksimovic, V. / Titman, S. (1991): Financial policy and reputation for product quality, Review of Financial Studies, 4 (1), 175-200

Metrick, A. / Yasuda, A. (2010): The Economics of Private Equity Funds, Review of Financial Studies, 23 (6), 2303-2341

Meuleman, M. / Wright, M. / Manigart, S. / Lockett, A. (2009): Private Equity Syndication: Agency Costs, Reputation and Collaboration, Journal of Business Finance & Accounting, 36 (5/6), 616-644

Miller, M. H. (1977): Debt and Taxes, Journal of Finance, 32 261-275

Modigliani, F. / Miller, M. H. (1958): The Cost of Capital, Corporation Finance and the Theory of Investment, American Economic Review, 48 (3), 261-297

Modigliani, F. / Miller, M. H. (1963): Corporate Income Taxes and the Cost of Capital: A Correction, American Economic Review, 53 433-443

Pindur, D. C. (2007): Value Creation in Successful LBOs, Wiesbaden 2007

Preqin Ltd. (2011): Early Warning System for LPs: Using Year Four/Six Performance Metrics to Predict Final Outcomes, Preqin Private Equity Performance Report, (March 2011), 1-6

Robinson, D. T. / Sensoy, B. A. (2010): Private Equity in the 21st Century: Cash Flows, Performance, and Contract Terms from 1984-2010, Working Paper Series, 1-51

Roden, D. M. / Lewellen, W. G. (1995): Corporate Capital Structure Decisions: Evidence from Leveraged Buyouts, Financial Management, 24 (2), 76-87

Stock, J. H. / Wright, J. H. / Yogo, M. (2002): A Survey of Weak Instruments and Weak Identification in Generalized Method of Moments, Journal of Business & Economic Statistics, 20 (4), 518-529

Strömberg, P. (2007): The new demography of private equity, Working Paper, 1-46

The Brattle Group (2011): 2009 Brattle Group Prize in Corporate Finance, http://www.brattle.com/NewsEvents/TheBrattleGroupPrizes.asp (2011-03-22)

Titman, S. (1984): The Effect of Capital Structure on a Firm's Liquidation Decision, Journal of Financial Economics, 13 (1), 137-151

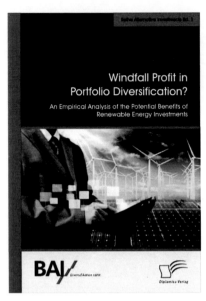

Frederik Bruns

Windfall Profit in Portfolio Diversification?

An Empirical Analysis of the Potential Benefits of Renewable Energy Investments

Diplomica 2013 / 112 Seiten / 39,50 Euro

ISBN 978-3-8428-8799-2
EAN 9783842887992

Modern Portfolio Theory is a theory which was introduced by Markowitz, and which suggests the building of a portfolio with assets that have low or, in the best case, negative correlation. In times of financial crises, however, the positive diversification effect of a portfolio can fail when Traditional Assets are highly correlated. Therefore, many investors search for Alternative Asset classes, such as Renewable Energies, that tend to perform independently from capital market performance.

'Windfall Profit in Portfolio Diversification?' discusses the potential role of Renewable Energy investments in an institutional investor's portfolio by applying the main concepts from Modern Portfolio Theory. Thereby, the empirical analysis uses a unique data set from one of the largest institutional investors in the field of Renewable Energies, including several wind and solar parks.

The study received the Science Award 2012 of the German Alternative Investments Association ('Bundesverband Alternative Investments e.V.').

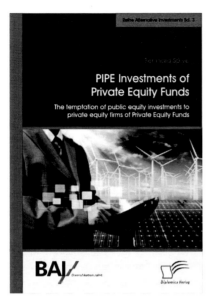

Bernhard Särve

PIPE Investments of Private Equity Funds

The temptation of public equity investments to private equity firms

Diplomica 2013 / 80 Seiten / 29,50 Euro

ISBN 978-3-8428-8911-8
EAN 9783842889118

Usually, private equity firms take control of firms which are privately held, and tend to act hidden. But, in recent years, the rising phenomenon of private investments in publicly listed companies, so-called PIPEs, could be observed. At first, this seems to be inconsistent but, it could become a perfect way to generate good returns.

This book gives an overview about the PIPE market, and then focuses on the role of private equity funds. How do they invest in publicly listed firms? And what are their motivations? Is the overall performance of PIPE deals superior to those of traditional private deals?

PIPE deals have much in common with typical venture capital deals with regard to the young and high-risk nature of target companies, and the minority ownership position. Surprisingly, buyout funds are relatively more engaged in PIPEs than venture funds are.

The author analyzes deal sizes, industry sectors, holding periods, IRRs and multiples of public deals, and comparable private deals with a unique data sample on transaction level. Finally, he discusses other possible motives for private equity firms to engage in these deals: improved liquidity, fast process of deal execution, access to certain markets, avoidance of takeover premiums and the thesis of an escape-strategy for surplus investment money.

Christina Halder

Finanzierung von M&A-Transaktionen

Vendor Loans und Earnout-Strukturen

Diplomica 2013 / 56 Seiten / 19,50 Euro

ISBN 978-3-8428-8913-2
EAN 9783842889132

Im Rahmen der Hochkonjunktur von M&A-Transaktionen beschäftigte sich eine große Anzahl von Experten aus Wissenschaft und Forschung mit den im M&A-Kontext aufkommenden Fragestellungen. Die vorliegende Untersuchung beschäftigt sich mit dem Thema der Finanzierung von M&A-Transaktionen durch den Verkäufer.
Die Zielsetzung besteht darin, die verschiedenen Möglichkeiten der Finanzierung von M&A-Deals durch den Verkäufer darzulegen. Es wird kritisch hinterfragt, welche Chancen eine derartige Lösung für die jeweilige Partei bietet und ob diese Chancen den möglichen Risiken überwiegen. Nach erfolgter Einführung in das Thema wird zunächst ein allgemeiner Überblick zu typischen Finanzierungsinstrumenten im Rahmen einer M&A-Transaktion gegeben. Es folgt eine Erläuterung zu den verschiedenen Möglichkeiten der Finanzierung des Kaufpreises durch den Verkäufer. Abschließend werden die aktuellen Entwicklungen auf dem M&A-Markt, insbesondere hinsichtlich der Finanzierungsstruktur von Transaktionen, beleuchtet, um zu erörtern, ob die Finanzierung durch den Verkäufer unter Annahme einer eingeschränkten, strengen Kreditvergabepolitik der Finanzinstitute zu einer Belebung des Transaktionsmarktes führen kann.